THE HOUSE THAT GOD BUILT

A Pictorial History of the Pokua-Ossei
Family of Koforidua, Ghana

MARTIN KWADWO OSSEI

AuthorHouse™ UK
1663 Liberty Drive
Bloomington, IN 47403 USA
www.authorhouse.co.uk
UK TFN: 0800 0148641 (Toll Free inside the UK)
UK Local: 02036 956322 (+44 20 3695 6322 from outside the UK)

Because of the dynamic nature of the Internet, any web addresses or links contained in this book may have changed
since publication and may no longer be valid. The views expressed in this work are solely those of the author and do not
necessarily reflect the views of the publisher, and the publisher hereby disclaims any responsibility for them.

Any people depicted in stock imagery provided by Getty Images are models,
and such images are being used for illustrative purposes only.
Certain stock imagery © Getty Images.

This book is printed on acid-free paper.

ISBN: 979-8-8230-9025-4 (sc)
ISBN: 979-8-8230-9027-8 (hc)
ISBN: 979-8-8230-9026-1 (e)

Library of Congress Control Number: 2024921590

Print information available on the last page.

Published by AuthorHouse 10/23/2024

authorHOUSE®

CONTENTS

FOREWORD 1

ACKNOWLEDGEMENTS 2

INTRODUCTION 4

Chapter 1   AWO AMA POKUA'S LIFE 7

Chapter 2   OBAAPANIN AFIA NYAME 16

Chapter 3   OBAAPANIN ABENA AKYAA 20

Chapter 4   OPANIN KWASI ANTUMI 23

Chapter 5   A SHORT HISTORY OF THE KOFORIDUA CATHOLIC CHURCH ... 25

Chapter 6   NANA ATUAHENE OF SANTROKOFI 29

Chapter 7   OBAAPANIN YAA TAKYIAW (MADAM AGNES OSSEI) ... 31

Chapter 8   HOUSE NUMBER K11 - OPANIN KWAME AFRAM (AKYEAMEHENE), AFIA SAKRA, ABENA KOBUA & MAAMA PAULO. 34

Chapter 9   ABUSUAPANIN KWASI NKRUMAH (SIR KNIGHT M. K. OSSEI, MASTER OSSEI) ... 38

Chapter 10   ABUSUAPANIN KWABENA OTI (SIR KNIGHT PROF KWABENA BOAKYE-YIADOM) ... 49

Chapter 11   AKWADUM CHRISTIAN VILLAGE 55

Chapter 12   KOFI'S STORY 63

Chapter 13   BORN AND BRED IN J47 66

Chapter 14   SERVING MY NATION AS A SOLDIER 68

Chapter 15   DR. ENO BOAKYE-YIADOM'S STORY 70

Chapter 16   A Word from Dr Josephine Owusu (nee Ossei), Ontario, Canada ... 72

Chapter 17   SPECIAL TRIBUTES 74

Chapter 18   WORDS OF WISDOM FROM LIVING ELDERS 82

Chapter 19   PHOTO GALLERY 90

Chapter 20   FAMILY DIRECTORY 104

FOREWORD

This book is aimed at putting on record the historical journey of one of the founding families of the great city of Koforidua, in the great country of Ghana. The country of Ghana has the enviable status of being the country closest to the centre of the earth, according to geographical maps. The Greenwich Meridian (North-South divide), passes through it and the Equator (East-West divide), runs just South of it, through the Gulf of Guinea. God created people and families and put the **Pokua-Ossei** family very close to the centre of the earth.

The beautiful city of Koforidua is in the southern part of Ghana, just 50 miles from the Gulf of Guinea. This history book, with pictures, is to give the reader, the story of one of the founding families of the city of Koforidua - **The Pokua-Ossei family**. The period covered is from the end of the 19th century to the present, 3rd decade of the 21st century.

It is a captivating read with personal stories interwoven with traditional history and a good sprinkling of photographs. Enjoy the story of the Pokua-Ossei family of Srodai, New Juaben, Ghana.

ACKNOWLEDGEMENTS

To ensure historical accuracy, this book was written on an open family platform with contributions from many family members. Our research was corroborated with known historical records.

The final editing of the book was done by an editorial team comprising Mrs Irene Owusu-Ansah (UK), Mr Anthony Owusu (Ghana), Dr Ralph Nyadu-Addo (Ghana), Ms Georgina Adwoa Pokua Frempong (Ghana), Mr Felix Kwabena Asiedu (USA) and Mr Michael Kofi Ossei (UK).

Thank you for your financial contribution towards the book: Anthony Ossei, Mrs Irene Owusu-Ansah, Martin Ossei, Dr Ralph Nyadu-Addo, Rev Michael Kwasi Ossei, Dr Josephine Owusu and Michael Kofi Ossei.

FOREWORD BY DAASEBRE NANA KWAKU BOATENG III, OMANHENE OF THE NEW JUABEN TRADITIONAL AREA.

The Pokua-Ossei Family has been one of the founding pillars of the New Juaben Traditional Area, of which I am the current paramount chief. They have been a very hard-working part of the New Juaben paramountcy since its foundation 150 years ago. They have led exemplarily in areas of Education, Christian spirituality, Politics and Business. My family and I are grateful beneficiaries of the leadership, love and community spirit of this family. I had the privilege of personally meeting Master Ossei (Mr M. K. Ossei), in his old age. I was impressed, even as a little child, with his dignity and humility. My mother would tell us many good stories about the Pokua-Ossei family. The family friendship has been strong from the beginning till now. I count on them as one of my most dependable and loyal advisors.

My prayer for the Pokua-Ossei family is that this book will motivate them to unite, work together for the good of the family, New Juaben and Ghana. Wherever the Pokua-Ossei family is, may they excel. May the close family bond between the Pokua-Ossei family and Yiadom-Hwedie royal family continue to blossom.

Daasebre Nana Kwaku Boateng lll
Omanhene of New Juaben Traditional Area

INTRODUCTION

In the year 1875, King Asafo Agyei of Juaben, Asante, had to flee from invading Asante forces and cross the River Pra, to safer grounds in Akyem territory, in present day Eastern region of Ghana.

A year before, in 1874, Asante empire forces had been defeated in the 'Sagrenti' war against the British colonial government, supported by troops from India, as well as tribal allies from Ghana, the Fantes and Denkyiras, and led by Sir Garnet Wolsley. This shook the Asante kingdom. as they had won two previous wars against the British colonial government. This time, the British introduced the machine gun, which was a game changer.

This led to the Asantehene, Kofi Karikari, being destooled and replaced by King Mensa Bonsu. Some Asante states, like Kokofu and Bekwai declared independence from the Asante alliance. Together with chiefs of Asokore, Affidwase and Nsuta, Juaben formed an independent kingdom, led by King Asafo Agyei of Juaben. It must be noted that Juaben was one of the biggest and strongest states in the Asante alliance. Juaben and Kumasi were the two strongest states in the alliance. With the king of Kumasi gaining the leadership of the Asante kingdom and enjoying the title of Asantehene, there was inevitable suspicion and occasional rivalry between the two, Kumasi and Juaben.

Juaben had been a self-standing kingdom for two centuries before the Asante grand alliance under King Osei Tutu, in the 1700s. At the height of its power, the Asante Kingdom covered almost all present-day Ghana, part of Cote D'Ivoire (the Ivory Coast) and part of the nation of Togo.

The Juaben king always played a vital role in the expansion the Asante kingdom. The confidence and strength of the Juaben nation posed a hidden challenge to the Asantehene, as happens in such alliances of strong men. In the 1830s, for instance, the Juabens, under King Kwasi Boateng, had crossed the Pra River, in self-exile, to enjoy the lavish hospitality of the Akyems, after a misunderstanding with Asantehene. The Juabens later returned from exile to their homeland in Asante when peace was restored with the Asantehene.

After the destoolment of King Kofi Karikari, and enstoolment of King Mensa Bonsu in Kumasi in 1874, King Mensah Bonsu was able to convince some of the new independent states to re-join the Asante alliance. Juaben, however, stood its ground and refused to re-join the alliance. Asante attacked and defeated Juaben, which necessitated the great exodus across the River Pra back into Akyem land, popularly referred to as '**Akwantu Kese**' by the Juabens, literally meaning, 'The Great Journey'.

On this journey, there was an Offinso royal, who would have been just a toddler or a little girl, called **AMA POKUA.** She is the grand matriarch and heroine of this book.

As **Ama Pokua** put her tiny hand into her Mum, Boatemaa's hand, as they began this hundred-mile plus journey on foot, little did she know that 150 years down the line, her grandchildren and great grandchildren will be celebrating her in a book. Her seed has multiplied. Her 'blood' now runs through the veins of many, old and young.

When she looks down from her lofty place in heaven, she would see clergy, educators, businessmen, doctors, nurses, soldiers, engineers, lawyers, civil servants, politicians and many other professions claiming to have enjoyed the milk from her breasts. Her descendants are spread out to all the continents on planet earth. We continue to multiply.

Enjoy the rich and enjoyable history and photos in this book. Long live the Pokua-Ossei family.

CHAPTER 1
AWO AMA POKUA'S LIFE

Nana Ama Pokua

Maame, Nana, Master

Nana Pokua House

Pokua farm lands

Daasebre Nana Kwaku Boateng II

Pokua family

As birth dating was not perfected, in Ghana, at the time of the birth of **Nana Ama Pokua**, we cannot give the accurate date of her birth. However, she died in March of 1958, as an elderly lady, of about 90 years. Assuming she was 90 years old then, this would mean that she was born in 1868, which would also mean that, she would have been 7 years old when the migration from Asante happened in 1875.

When Nana Asafo Agyei and the Juabens moved down south, the chief of Kukurantumi, encouraged by Okyehene of the time, Nana Amoako Atta 1, gave them land in present day Koforidua, to settle. As happens in all migrations, some settled along the way, and did not make it as far as Koforidua. They founded towns like Enyiresi, Kankan, Asaman, Osiem and others. It was only in the 1920s that Okyehene, Nana Ofori Atta 1, persuaded the British government to direct all settlements in Akyem

Abuakwa and Akyem Kotoku to change their allegiance to Okyehene. Before then, these towns were Asante settler towns with Juaben connection.

Koforidua however became the independent paramountcy of New Juaben. The New Juaben chief was an independent Omanhene (Paramount chief). However, due to family ties with those who remained in Asante Juaben, there remained an affiliation and cooperation between New and Old Juaben. The relationship between these two was dependent on the sentiment of the ruling monarchs.

When the final big group of migrants arrived in present day Koforidua, **Nana Ama Pokua** and her family settled around the area, that houses the present-day Koforidua Community Centre and Koforidua Methodist Cathedral. Other notable families that settled there were the Brukus, Asante Tanos, Asamoahs, Osei-Hwedies and others, who have all become strong pillars in New Juaben today. It may be of some importance to note that the name, **Koforidua**, is said to have originated from that area where Nana Ama Pokua and her family first settled.

History tells us that: A man called Kofi Ofori had a rest stop, underneath a giant mahogany tree, in that same area. Travellers would stop for rest and refreshment at this rest stop. It became a popular landmark and meeting point. "Hyia me wo Koo Fori dua no ase" (Meet me under Koo Fori's tree). This evolved into Koforidua.

The area where the family settled is also called **Srodai**. It is surely the cradle of the Koforidua township. Most of the original families settled there and, together with the adjoining suburb of **Betom**, you will find the family homes of most of the original settlers. The Omanhene's palace is located in Srodai, and many of the town elders have their family homes in these two areas.

The early settlers were mainly farmers. **Nana Ama Pokua** was a farmer. They had been given a large piece of land by the Okyehene, and it stood to reason that one had to farm to survive. In those days, the main occupations were farming and trading. They had been given a large expanse of land and one could farm as big a land as they could manage, we are told. The more hands you had, the bigger the land you could cultivate. Families united in farming co-operatives. Having many children was a great advantage as it brought in more hands for farming. Polygamy was a common practice then and it was not uncommon to have women with multiple fathers for their children. Having children was a big priority, partly for economic reasons.

Nana Pokua had nine children. We know this for a fact, because her last-born was named, Kwasi Nkrumah. Nkrumah is the name given to the ninth born. We have no trace of four her children, so can't tell you anything on them for now, but we will feature each of the five, that we have information on, in later chapters of this book.

It is very important to note that, at this point in the history of Juaben, there was acute shortage of men due to the many wars they fought. The Juaben king, Akwasi Boateng, for instance was given the title, "OWOROKOMA" which means, the dependable one in battle, by the Asantehene, when he, together with the Kontenase chief, went to retrieve the golden stool from the British. During the Akatamanso war with the British in 1826. Otumfuo, Osei Yaw Akoto had retreated from the battlefield in the face of heavy onslaught by the enemy. The British gained possession of the revered golden stool of the Asante kingdom. The Juabenhene and Kuntenasehene were the two kings who were said to have led their forces to retrieve the priced stool. These were high casualty wars, where many men were lost in battle. In 1832, there was a misunderstanding between the Asantehene and Juabenhene. Accusations and counteraccusations ended in a war. The Asantehene was Nana Osei Yaw Akoto. Juabenhene was Nana Kwasi Boateng. Nana Kwasi Boateng moved to Akyem for the first time, when the Asantehene invaded Juaben.

Kwasi Boateng died in exile in Saman, near Osino. His brother, who succeeded him, also died eighty days after, and there was no man in the royal family to succeed him. When Asantehene, Osei Yaw Akoto, died in 1834, Juaben returned to their homeland in Old Juaben from Akyem, led by a woman, Queen Ama Serwaa (Juaben Serwaa), who ruled as Juabenhene. Ama Serwaa was succeeded by her daughter Ohemaa Afrakoma in 1846, who in turn was succeeded by her daughter, Akua Sarpomaa.

King Asafo Agyei, who led the 'Akwantu Kese' (the great pilgrimage) to Koforidua, was the husband of Akua Sarpomaa. Asafu Agyei was also the son of Juabenhene, Kwasi Boateng, who died at Saman. Nana Asafo Agyei was declared Juabenhene by Asantehene, though his royalty was through his father (patrilineal), but Asante inheritance law is matrilineal (through the mother). Asafo Agyei's father was a king of Juaben, but strict customary law would have disqualified him. His wife, the queen, was the legitimate heir according to Asante custom. However, Asafo Agyei had a lot of influence, and with the backing of his wife was declared Juabenhene.

Another reason why Asafo Agyei made enemies with some of the chiefs in Asante was that he belonged to the **Asona** clan. The clans are big family units who traced their ancestry to the same ancestor in history.

There are 8 clans or original family groups in Asante. They are Oyoko, Bretuo, Agona, Asona, Asenie, Aduana, Ekuona and Asakyiri. King Osei Tutu, the founder of the Asante Kingdom was an Oyoko.

The Juaben stool had been occupied by members of the **Oyoko** clan. It is an Oyoko stool. Asafo Agyei, occupying it meant, the stool had been transferred to another family. He got a lot of opposition from the Oyoko clan states in Asante, including Kumasi. This made him quite angry with Asante.

Our grandmother, **Nana Pokua** was of the Asona clan and an Offinso royal. Offinso is one of the Asona stools in Asante. These clans are the same in all the Akan areas, therefore making the Akans, one big family. The Okyenhene, king of Akyem, is considered head of all the Asonas. One of his titles is **"Asona Piesie"**. King Asafo Agyei was technically the 'brother' of the Okyenhene. It is said, they had a very close relationship. This explains the great hospitality Akyem offered the travelling Juabens under the Asona king.

When Juaben settled in Koforidua, new families were brought into the chieftaincy of the area, while still maintaining some of the old bloodlines. There was the need for reorganisation to suit the new reality.

The Akyeamehene stool (chief of Srodai) went to the extended family of our grandmother, **Nana Pokua.** Women were very powerful in those days. We are told that when the men went to war in Asante, **Nana Ama Pokua** sat as Akyeamehene, settling disputes and performing all the functions of a chief.

It must be noted that many in New Juaben had relatives in Old Juaben. Some Juaben chiefs were close to Asante, others were not that close. 'New Juaben' men, often went to support their relatives in 'Old Juaben' in times of war. In 1901, the real ruler of Koforidua, Queen Ama Serwaa, left Koforidua to settle in Old Juaben and the Koforidua stool was left in the hands of caretaker Chiefs Okyere and Asafo Boateng. Asafo Boateng, who was of the Krontihene lineage in old Juaben, later became the substantive Juaben king and ruled for many years.

When the British colonial government wanted to build bridges with Asante, they felt King Asafo Agyei, who led the Juabens from Asante, stood in their way, because of his anger against Asante, so they sent him into exile in Lagos, Nigeria in 1880, where he died. The colonial government knew the power of Asanteman and didn't want to get on a wrong foot with them. King Asafo Agyei's bitterness was standing in the way of trying to build bridges with Asante.

Nana Pokua was respected by the Koforidua community, including the chiefs. The Pokua house in Srodai has been a mentoring ground for many royals of the Koforidua stool. **Nana Kwaku Boateng II**, one of the most revered chiefs of Koforidua, spent a considerable time living in the Nana Pokua family house, to help prepare him for his duties as Omanhene. Nana Kwaku Boateng II was enstooled as Omanhene of New Juaben in 1962, after the death of Nana Akrasi. He ruled as Omanhene of New Juaben, until his death in 1990

Nana Pokua's first child, Afia Nyame, was born to a man from the Debrah family of Debrah Krom. Her second child, Abena Akyaa, comes from the Darko family of I. K. Darko, Koforidua Motel. His other children, we have knowledge of are Kwasi Antumi, Yaa Takyiaw (Obaa Panyin Agnes Ossei), and her last born was Kwasi Nkrumah (Sir Knight M. K. Ossei, Master Ossei).

Nana Pokua would have been among the early Christian converts of the Methodists in Koforidua. As the Methodists first came to Koforidua, with missionaries from Aburi in 1884, they were given a piece of land around the same area where **Nana Pokua's** family house was. She would have been an early convert for the Methodist missionaries, as her first born was called, Afia Nyame. Nyame means God. The family was Methodist until Kwasi Antumi, one of her sons, married Maame Akosua Abon of the Asante household, of Koforidua Social Welfare area in Srodai. Akosua Abon's father, Mr Charles Asante, was one of the pioneers of the Catholic Church in Koforidua, as the Catholics made an entry into Koforidua in 1911. Later, the Pokua Ossei household would play a very central role in the Catholic Church in Koforidua, and in Ghana as a whole. Nana Ama Pokua died in March, 1958.

CHAPTER 2
OBAAPANIN AFIA NYAME

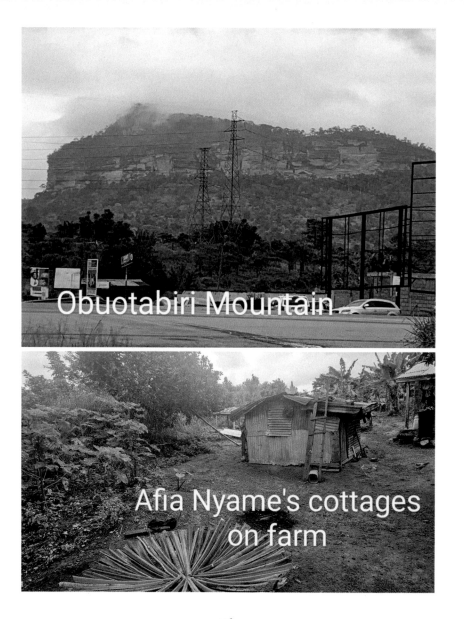

Obuotabiri Mountain

Afia Nyame's cottages
on farm

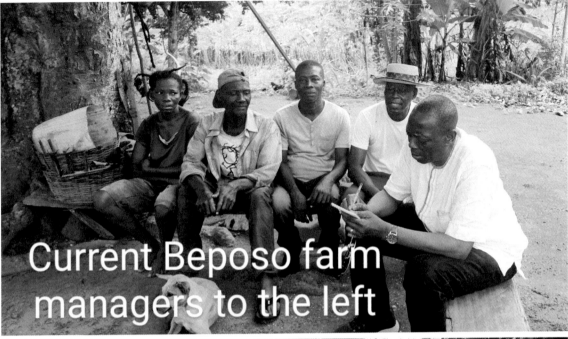

Current Beposo farm managers to the left

Kwae3mu Resort

OBAAPANIN AFIA NYAME (Awo a ote akuraa) was the first born of Nana Pokua. She was born around 1894. She was christened Joanna Debrah at her baptism into the Christian faith. She died in 1976 at the age of about 82. Her father was from the Debrah family and was from the same father as the famous I. K. Debrah, bookseller and estate developer, of Debrakrom fame. She was a dedicated farmer and spent most of her life living near the farms, in the farm cottages. This is what gave her the nick name, Awo a ote akuraa, literally meaning, old lady who lives in the village.

The family had extensive farmlands on the lower parts of the Obuotabiri mountain. There were large fertile lands around the mountain, and it was prime land for the new settlers. Nana Pokua and her family had farms there. They established a small village, near the farms which became a home, away from home. **Awo Afia Nyame** loved farming so much that she made this farming settlement, her permanent home. She only visited the family home in Srodai occasionally. She visited the rest of the family on special occasions, for church services and when she needed hospital care. Though the structures have changed a little, the cottages Awo Afia Nyame called home, still stand.

The Nana Pokua family remained farmers, even when family members took on other employment. Saturdays were always times to visit **Awo** on the farms and bring some food back home. **Awo,** would be excited to see the family at the farm, and would cook for the whole family. Her speciality was Akaw (cocoyam cooked in the skin) and Kontomire stew (cocoyam leaves stew, with palm oil and dried fish). In the rainy season, the 'Adebon lake' next to the farm cottages, will spring to life, full of water, and the family could enjoy a refreshing swim. This was heaven to the kids.

Saturday was farm day. Several family groups from Koforidua would be climbing up the hill to their own farms on Saturday. There was the buzz of a festival, as families travelled together to their various farms on the lower heights of the Obuotabiri mountain. Coming back was not as enjoyable, as each person, even children, would be carrying a headload of food. Every child in the family would be waiting for the day when they would be mature enough to join on the Saturday family trip to the Beposo (mountain top) farm.

The Pokua family still owns extensive land on the slopes of the **Obuotabiri Mountain**. The Obuotabiri Mountain is not just an imposing landmark but plays a significant role in the lives of the people of Koforidua.

The Obuotabiri Mountain is part of the Akuapem-Kwahu scarp. It is a beautiful mountain of arranged rocks, which rises above the Koforidua township, like a grand overseer of the town. It is no wonder, some of the town folk regard it as a god. The name Obuotabiri means the rock of Tabiri. Tabiri being the name of the deity that occupies the rock. It is the main deity of the New Juaben stool. The Akyems, before, worshipped it as a god, and the Juabens inherited this worship. It was not uncommon for mountains to be worshipped as gods, as the height of the mountains made them closer to 'the great god of the sky'. This deity was served by dwarfs, and its main priest was the 'Obuotabiri priestess', who made sacrifices on behalf of the state, several times a year. Tabiri's followers believed, he strengthened them in war, made barren women fruitful, and helped them to have bumper harvests.

The Obuotabiri mountain is now a big tourist attraction, with new buildings springing up, encroaching on the farmlands and serene settlements of **Afia Nyame's** time. Several Telecom masts have also been erected on the mountain, due of its height and convenience. **Kwae3mu Resort** has been established by a Pokua Ossei family member, to provide rest and refreshment, halfway up the mountain top, for tourist and joggers. The mountain has also become a popular destination for fitness walks.

Awo Afia Nyame (Joanna Debrah), moved to the family home in Srodai in her final years, where she died peacefully in 1976 at the age of 82.

CHAPTER 3
OBAAPANIN ABENA AKYAA

Maame Cecilia Frempong

Papa Gabriel Frempong & volunteers building St George's

Frempong sisters

Adwoa, Adarkwa, Badu

OBAA PANIN ABENA AKYAA (Awo a ote fie), was Nana Pokua's second daughter. She was the older sister of the late I. K. Darko, of Koforidua Motel fame, from the same father. Their father was Hackman from Obosomase in Akuapem. The family referred to **Abena Akyaa** as 'Awo a ote fie', literally meaning, 'Old Lady who lives in the house'. She lived in the family home till she passed on at a good old age.

Awo was a farmer like the rest of the family. She farmed on family lands on the Koforidua-Mamfe Road. Her farm was around present-day Galloway junction, where the present Koforidua Cultural Centre and International Central Gospel Church are located. It is most encouraging to think that a Church and a cultural centre would have been built where **Awo Abena Akyaa** farmed. **Awo Abena Akyaa,** like the rest of the Pokua family, was a Christian convert committed to the worship of the Lord Jesus Christ.

Awo was a very kind and generous person, loved dearly by the Pokua household, especially the children. All the children looked forward to her regular 'Afabaawom' meal, prepared for all the children of the household. Afabaawom was a pot-mix of cocoyam, yam, vegetables and fish. All the children in the house would arrange their plates in a long line, cheerfully waiting for their plates to be served by Awo. Awo Abena Akyaa had her favourites among the children, who were entitled to a slightly bigger portion. All the children of the family would strive to be of good behaviour, so they would get in Awo's good books, because the Afabaawom was a delicious treat.

Awo Abena Akyaa, gave birth to **Maame Afia Brenya** (Cecilia Frempong, Maame Anya). Maame Anya's given name at her baptism into the Christian faith was **Cecilia Saaneye**. She took on her husband's surname, Frempong when she got married to her husband, **Gabriel Frempong.** Afia Boatemaa was Maame Anya's birth name. Brenya (literally meaning 'struggle to get'), was a nick name given to her because of her mother's struggle to have children.

Afia Brenya (popularly known as Maame Anya), married **Papa Kwame To** (Gabriel Frempong), a well-respected farmer who later became a blacksmith, noted for his ability to make special keys and guns. He was well known in the Srodai Community as the preferred blacksmith and handyman. His house and workshop were right in the centre of Srodai. Papa Kwame To was one of the enthusiastic pioneers of the Koforidua Catholic Church. He was a leading volunteer in the construction of the twin tower St Georges Catholic Church, in the hills, behind the Omanhene's palace.

It is said that Nana Pokua was so impressed with **Gabriel Frempong**'s work ethic and farming ability that, she was determined to have him as a son-in-law and wooed him for her granddaughter, Afia Brenya. Papa Gabriel Frempong and Afia Brenya had 12 children. Their first born, **Kwabena Agyekum** (John Maxwell Frempong), was a popular draughtsman and civil servant in Koforidua. He also sang the lead bass in the St. Georges Catholic Choir. Other children were **Adwoa Agyeiwaa** (Mary Okyere, Teacher Mary), **Joseph Kofi Adarkwah-Yiadom**, who later moved to the U.K. and is the Abusua Panin of the Pokua family in the UK, then **Yaw Manu**. He was followed by **Akua Nyantakyiwaa** (Theresa Oppong, Baby Panin**), Akua Boatemaa** (Anna Frempong, Baby Ketewa), **Kwadwo Aboagye** (Martin Frempong, Kwadwo Panin), **Abena Frempomaa** (Rosemary Frempong), **Abena Boadiwaa** (Kate Badu Frempong), **Akua Duku Mansah** and **Georgina Adwoa Pokua Frempong**, named after Nana Pokua.

Anthony Kwasi Owusu

Anthony Owusu

Michael Owusu

Augustine Owusu

Rev Fr Owusu Frempong

OPANIN KWASI ANTUMI is the middle child of Ama Pokua's 5 children that we have record of. Not much is known of **Kwasi Antumi,** because he died at a very young age, though he left a remarkable legacy in the family. He was known to have possessed great physical strength. He won many boxing contests in his time.

Kwasi Antumi, married Akosua Abon of the Asante family, whose family house is in the Social Welfare area of Srodai. Akosua Abon's father, Charles Asante, was one of the founding members of the Catholic Church in Koforidua. This marriage was what facilitated the Pokua family's move from the Methodist to the Catholic Church. The Pokua family became strong pillars in the Koforidua Catholic Church. Kwasi Antumi's legacy was that he brought two strong Christian families together, through marriage. The history of the Catholic Church in Koforidua and the Eastern Region of Ghana would not be complete without the mention of the Ossei and Asante families.

Kwasi Antumi died before his son, **Kwasi Duah** (Anthony Kwasi Owusu), formerly of the ministry of Agriculture and Cocoa board, was old enough to know him. **Opanin Antumi's** first grandson is **Anthony Owusu**, a retired civil servant, who has played a strong part in the Koforidua Catholic Church. Other children of Kwasi Duah are Anna Owusu, Augustine Michael Owusu, Regina Owusu, Rev Father Samuel Owusu Frempong and Michael Owusu. The rest are Christiana Owusu Yeboah, Isaac Owusu, Agnes Yaa Owusu, Agnes Owusu Boamah., Dominic Kwadwo Asante Owusu, Michael Kwasi Owusu, Vivian Amma Owusu, Raphael Yaw Owusu, Gabriel Osei Owusu, Rosemond Owusu-Dankwa, Regina Mida Owusu, Lucinda Takyiaw Owusu, Philomena Owusu and Agnes Owusu.

Anthony Kwasi Duah Owusu did a lot of his agricultural field work in the Akyem Abuakwa area and extended the Pokua-Ossei family influence into Akyem Abuakwa. His son, **Reverend Father Samuel Owusu Frempong** was ordained into the priesthood of the Catholic Church in 1992.

CHAPTER 5
A SHORT HISTORY OF THE KOFORIDUA CATHOLIC CHURCH

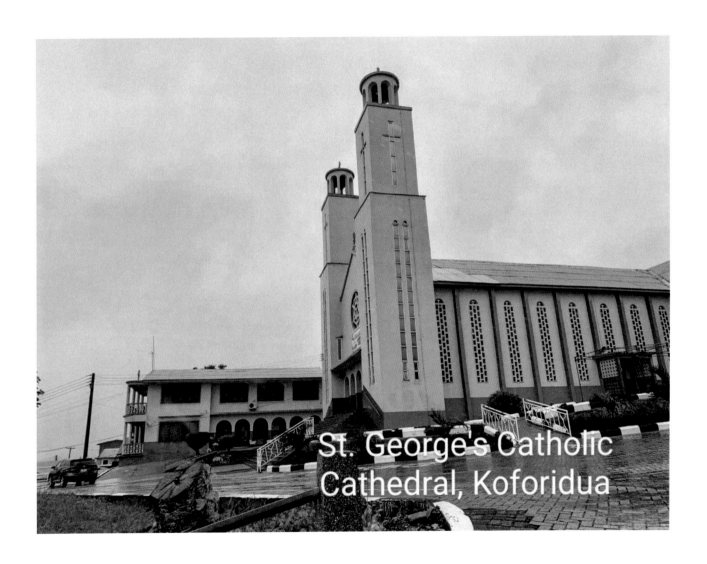

St. George's Catholic Cathedral, Koforidua

Mr Sylvester B. Osabutey, a Catholic from German Togoland, is one of the first names associated with the establishment of the Koforidua Catholic Church. As Koforidua was a cocoa producing and commercial centre, many travellers from other parts of Ghana and beyond, converged there for business. Mr Osabutey was one such immigrant, who helped to start a Catholic group under a tent in Anwona (Ewe) Town. Mr. Osabutey's group was affiliated with the Keta Catholic Church when they started. The first baptism of three infants was conducted in 1913, which became the official start date of the Catholic Church in Koforidua. As the Church grew, the affiliation was moved from Keta to Cape Coast, and later to the Accra mission. The Church grew until they approached **Daasebre Nana Kwaku Boateng 1**, Omanhene of New Juaben, who gave them land to build in the centre of Srodai. This land where they built the first church, now houses the Catholic basic school complex, near the place formerly known as 'Ocansey'. This was a hilly water-logged undulating land, but the church worked to level the place to put up their building in 1924. They had their first resident priest, Father Lemens SMA (Society of African Missions), take post about 3 years later. He also had responsibility for all other parts of the Eastern Region. There were very few priests at the time with most of them, missionaries from other nations. In 1941, the SVD (Divine Word Mission), took over from the SMA in Accra, and posted Rev Fr Alphonse Erlsbend, assisted by Rev Fr Anthony Bauer to Koforidua.

Rev Fr Anthony Bauer supervised the building of the still standing twin tower, **St Georges Cathedral**, and Rev Fr Henry Jansenn added the priest's house. The SVD society established **the Mount Mary Teacher Training College** at Agormanya, near Somanya in 1947, to train teachers to feed its basic schools. Mr M. K Ossei (Master Ossei) was one of its founding teachers. They offered 4-year teacher Training Course for 'Teacher's Certificate A' and a 2-year course for 'Teacher's Certificate B'. One of Master Ossei's proteges, the celebrated Lawyer A. K. Adu Amankwaa, also from Srodai, became the first African Vice Principal of the school. The SVD also founded **St Peter's Secondary School** at Nkwatia, Kwahu in 1957.

Rev. Fr. Alphonse Erlsbend, who was Principal of Mount Mary Training College, Agormanya, moved to become the first principal of **St John's Secondary and Minor Seminary**, which was established at Effiduase, New Juaben, and opened on 21st January 1958. The school later changed its name to **Pope**

John Secondary School when it became a government assisted school in 1968. The name change was to differentiate it from other Catholic Schools bearing the 'St John's' name in the country.

The role of the Catholic Church in the education and health of the residents of New Juaben and the Eastern Region has been immense. The Pokua-Ossei family has been in the centre of this education and health revolution. Aside several primary and middle schools established by the Koforidua St Georges Catholic Church, Madonna International School was also established in 1966, to provide quality, world class primary education.

The medical Brothers of St John of God, another Catholic Missionary society, established the **St Joseph's Hospital**, also in Effiduase, and next to Pope John's Secondary School, in 1959. This hospital has grown to be one of the best hospitals in Ghana for Orthopaedic surgery. The Dominican Sisters established St Dominic's Hospital at Akwatia in 1960. St Dominic's is the biggest Christian run Hospital in Ghana and is overseen by the Koforidua Catholic Diocese. The Dominican Sisters added St Roses Secondary Shool in 1965. St Martin's Secondary School in Nsawam began in 1966. Wherever you see any Catholic project in the New Juaben and Eastern Region area, there is surely the hand of a Pokua-Ossei in it.

The history of the Catholic Church in Koforidua cannot be concluded without mentioning the grand **50 years golden jubilee celebration of the Catholic Church in 1963**, led by Rev Theodore Van Eyndhoven (SVD). It had the theme **"That All May Be One"**. It was a great and unforgettable festival that brought Catholic Clergy and members from the whole nation of Ghana to celebrate the goodness of God and the oneness of the Church. All roads led to Koforidua for this Catholic festival. Our family played a leadership role in this celebration.

Koforidua Catholic Church was elevated to a diocese in 1992. Bishop Charles Palmer Buckle served as its first bishop from 1992 to 2005. He was succeeded in 2006 to the present, by Bishop Joseph Afrifa-Agyekum. These are two popular bishops who have continued to push the work of the Catholic Church in the region.

Family Photo

CHAPTER 6

NANA ATUAHENE OF SANTROKOFI

Alice & Kwabena Atuahene

NANA ATUAHENE was an adopted son of Ama Pokua. He was a royal from Santrokofi, in the Volta Region, who would have been given as a gift to the family of Nana Ama Pokua. The Asante kingdom, at the time, extended to parts of present-day Volta Region of Ghana. It was not uncommon, in those days, to have royals of conquered states brought back to be trained in the royal houses of the conquerors. Nana Atuahene was one of such royals.

The Asante army invaded the whole area from Nkonya to Buem in 1870, under the command of General Adu Bofour. It is not uncommon to find people from Santrokofi with links to New Juaben, as the Juaben chief was one of the generals of the Asante army. **Nana Atuahene** became one of the children of Nana Pokua and stayed in the Pokua household until his death at a grand old age. His children relocated to Santrokofi after his death but have maintained the relationship with the Pokua-Ossei family and attend family functions and funerals in the Pokua family home in Koforidua.

Family @ home (J47)

CHAPTER 7
OBAAPANIN YAA TAKYIAW (MADAM AGNES OSSEI)

Maame Yaa

Madam Agnes Ossei
(Maame Yaa)

Maame Yaa, Meefa
(Ama Sefa), children &
grandchildren

Daasebre on family visit

Yaa Takyiaw, was also fondly called, Maame Yaa or Maame Panin, by his children, grand-children and other members of the family. She was born in 1914, as the eighth child of Nana Pokua. She was a child of Nana Pokua's latter years. After the 7th child, Kwasi Antumi was born, there was a gap in years before **Maame Yaa** and later, **Kwasi Nkrumah** (Master Ossei), were born. Her father was **Opanin Osei** from Aboaso in Asante, who was a popular 'Odunsini' (herbalist) in the New Juaben area.

Maame Yaa was a respected trader and businesswoman in the community. She was also a farmer like her other siblings. She was hailed as one of the most beautiful women in the community. Her cosmetic and toiletries stall was right in the middle of the central aisle of the Koforidua Central Market. Her store was in the 'centre of the centre' of the market. This gives an indication of how influential she was in the community.

Together with her younger brother, M. K. Ossei, they positively influenced the lives of many families in Koforidua, through their charitable and mentoring work. **Maame Yaa** inherited the position of **Obaa**

Panin (matriarch) of the family, on the death of her mother. Her older living sisters, Afia Nyame and Abena Akyaa, were also quite elderly and concentrated on their farming.

Maame Yaa was a very generous woman. Family and friends benefited generously from her business. She made sure we were all looking creamed up and smelling nice from her beauty shop. Some of us children who had to travel to boarding schools, away from home, could count on some cosmetics like S-curl, Vaseline, powder, soaps and other things as gifts from her shop.

She was open and welcoming. Her sitting room in the Pokua house, was an open room for all of us in the house. Everyone was welcome in her apartment in the Pokua House. In fact, the main switch for the outside light, that gave light to the common area of the house, **J 47**, was in her sitting room. When it starts getting dark, you would hear shouts of 'aasoo light' (corruption of 'outside light') meaning, it was time to turn on the outside light. Any child could run in **Maame Yaa's** room and turn on the light. If you were one of her favourites, you could receive a piece of bread or biscuit, if she was in her room.

Maame Yaa, like other members of the Nana Ama Pokua household, was a dedicated Christian of the Catholic Church and played her role creditably in the Koforidua St. Georges Catholic Church. She was a leading member of the Christian Mothers Association and of the St. Anthony's Guild. When **Maame Panin** passed on to be with the Lord in 1993, it was the renowned Catholic Archbishop, **Peter Akwasi Sarpong**, from Kumasi Diocese, who travelled all the way from Kumasi, to lead her wake service in Koforidua. This spoke of her extended influence.

The first of Maame **Yaa's** 7 children was **Akua Poraba** (Elisabeth Reinduls, Ante Akua), then **Afia Manu** (Veronica Reinduls, Sister). After that, **Kwabena Oti** (Professor K. Boakye-Yiadom), then **Yaa Asantewa** (Philomena Boakye, Ante Yaa), **Akua Ago** (Joana Boakye, Sister Ago), **Akosua Gyamfua** (Margaret Bannor, Ante Maggie) and **Serwa Barnie** (Mary Banahene, Sister Barnie).

Maame Yaa rested peacefully with the Lord at the age of 79, on May 17th, 1993.

CHAPTER 8
HOUSE NUMBER K11 - OPANIN KWAME AFRAM (AKYEAMEHENE), AFIA SAKRA, ABENA KOBUA & MAAMA PAULO.

Madam Rosina Osei (Ante Adwoa)

Maame Afia Sakra

Family funeral in London

The famous house number **K11** of Srodai was the next house to **J47**, the main **Nana Ama Pokua** family home. In the old days, there were no brick walls separating the two houses, and the family in both households lived very closely together. K11 was occupied by cousins, nephews and nieces of Nana Ama Pokua. This chapter is dedicated to some notable names from K11.

The history of K11 is traced back to **Akua Akyamaa (Akua Dei)** who was the daughter of Biyaa, who would have been part of the journey from Old Juaben to New Juaben (Akwantu Kese). Akua Adei became Obaa Panin of the extended family after the death of Nana Ama Pokua. **Awo Afia Nyame** is remembered as being the carer by Akua Dei's bedside in her last days, as she was the next oldest sister. Awo Afia Nyame who lived on the farms at Beposo was known for her caring nature and moved to stay close to Awo Akua Akyamaa to serve her during her last days on earth.

Akua Akyamaa was also called Akua Dei because she was born during the Awukudae festival.

*The 'Adae' festivals of the Asantes are holidays when the people of Asante rested from work and spent time celebrating their chiefs, remembering ancestors and making sacrifices to their gods. This was done on specially chosen Wednesdays (**Awukudae**) and Sundays (**Akwasidae**).*

Akua Dei gave birth to **Kwabena Owusu, Kwame Afram, Afia Boatemaa (Afia Sakra), Abena Kobuah (Maa Abena) and Maama Paulo**.

Kwabena Owusu died young while **Kwame Afram** (JB Scatter) became **Akyeamehene** (chief of Srodai), New Juaben. Opanin Afram was the father of **Comfort Amoah** (Bobosey), **Ama Boatemaa, Akosua Dei, Comfort Yaa Boatemaa Amoah, Godfred Kwadwo Amoah Panin, Joyce Amoah Panin, James Atta Panin Owusu, James Atta Kakra Owusu**.

Afia Sakra, Maa Abena and Maama Paulo were pillars in the Srodai community. Afia Sakra was the mother of **Rosina Osei** (Adwoa Agyapomaa), **Comfort Boadi-Asiedu** (nee Danso), **Samuel Kofi Addo** and **Eric Yaw Korade Tetteh**.

Maa Abena's children were **Irene Okrah** (Auntie Ama), **Kwaku Okra**, **Kwabena Fosu**, **Kwasi Boateng** (Okyenasco), **Morgan Asante** and **Akosua Boahemaa**.

Maama Paulo's children were **Eddie Asante, Charles Asante, Paul Asante** and **Sampson Atta Asante.**

Akyeamehene **Kwasi Afram** died in August 1969 at the age of 69. Afia Sakra died at the ripe age of 95 years in September 2006 and her younger sister, Maa Abena joined her sister in eternity on 6th March 2007 at 93 years old. The descendants of **K11** continue to multiply and flourish all over the world.

CHAPTER 9
ABUSUAPANIN KWASI NKRUMAH (SIR KNIGHT M. K. OSSEI, MASTER OSSEI)

Sir Knight M. K. Ossei

Mama Alexcia in Church

Ossei Fie (Asaasim).
MK lived here.

Sir Knight

Lizzie, George, Philo

The Wedding

Abusua Panin Kwasi Owusu Agyeman

Can you spot Bishop Palmer Buckle?

Joseph Adolphus &
Rebecca Pat-Williams
& family

Mama Alexcia & choir
leaders

MK the negotiator

MK back from prison

Honoured by the Pope

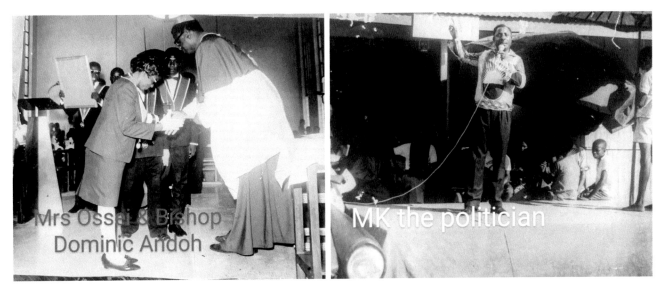

Mrs Ossei & Bishop Dominic Andoh

MK the politician

Family photo (early 1970s)

Kwasi Nkrumah was the 9th child and last born of Nana Ama Pokua. He shared the same father, Agya Osei from Aboaso, with his immediate older sister, Yaa Takyiaw. As the one male child of Nana Pokua. who lived to full adulthood, he was saddled with the responsibility of leading the family as Abusua Panin (family head), from a very young age. He performed this role creditably and has positively influenced the lives of many.

Michael Kwasi Ossei was born in July 1918 and had his early basic education at the Koforidua Methodist School. He was exposed to the Catholic Church, through one of his siblings, Kwasi Antumi. He became a faithful servant and pillar in the Catholic Church in New Juaben and Ghana, as he devoted his life to the service of God.

The early Catholic missionaries found, in this intelligent and enthusiastic boy, a great community asset and committed to a mutually beneficial relationship which lasted till **Master Ossei's** departure from this earth in 1982.

He was one of the first Catholics in Ghana to be honoured with the '**Knight of St Gregory**' award. Wikipedia describes this award as "*The honour bestowed upon Catholic men and women (and certain notable non-Catholics) in recognition of their personal service to the Holy See and to the Catholic Church, through their unusual labours, their support of the Holy See, and the examples they set in their communities and their countries.*"

Paapa, as the family fondly calls him, was given this Papal knighthood with the title of **Sir Knight**. This recognition was officiated by the celebrated **Rt. Rev. Bishop Dominic Andoh** of the Accra Diocese, and during the watch of the hard-working **Rev. Fr. Frederick Hahn** of the St. George's Parish, Koforidua

One of the first changes, his association with the Catholic missionaries brought into **Paapa Ossei's** life was that he was made to adopt his father's name, Osei, as his surname. This was not a customary practice of the Asantes. It was a European practice which was introduced to the new converts. Paapa's given name at birth was, **Kwasi Owusu Agyeman**. The second change was that the foreign missionaries spelt his name

With a double 'ss'. This would enable them to pronounce his name rightly, with emphasis on the second part of the name. **Kwasi Nkrumah Owusu Agyeman** was christened **Michael Kwasi Ossei.**

Paapa M. K. Ossei was encouraged to attend the flagship Catholic College, St. Augustine's College in Cape Coast, which had been founded a few years before, in 1930. He was sent there to train as a teacher. This would turn out to be a master stroke by the missionaries, as Paapa's greatest legacy would be, as an educator. He ran the Catholic school complex in Srodai for many years. Many have passed through his educational supervision. All over Koforidua, from **Srodai** to **Betom to Anwona town**, **Zongo** and **Nsukwao**, the **Koforidua Catholic Primary and Middle schools** were their school of choice. The school still stands at its original location, still producing world changers.

Everyone knew '**Master Ossei'.** He treated everyone as family, as he was operating on family ground. There was not one household in Srodai that did not have a member attending Koforidua Catholic School. The school was right in the middle of Srodai. Most of the royal family of New Juaben attended this school. **Master,** as he was fondly called in the community, ensured that every child in the area was encouraged to be educated. He offered opportunities to the local women to be food sellers and engage in other profitable ventures in and around the school. He would mobilise schoolteachers and students, where necessary, to be of help to the community in voluntary community enhancing projects. He was the grand uncle and family counsellor to the whole community.

Master Ossei spearheaded the establishment of Catholic schools in **Effiduase, Asokore, Oyoko**, **Suhyen, Nyirede** and other communities around Koforidua. Most of these schools were headed by **Master Ossei's** former students, who themselves had become trained educators. He was a central part of the establishment of Pope John's Secondary School in 1958 (formerly St John's Secondary and Minor Seminary). He was also instrumental in the establishment of Madonna International School.

He did not only chair several boards facilitating these projects, **but Master Ossei** also raised funds through fund-raising projects and organised 'walatu walasa' (voluntary labour) to physically help build these facilities. He was one of the first teachers at Mount Mary Training College, Agormanya.

This was the first Catholic Training College for teachers in the Eastern Region of Ghana. Mount Mary was founded in 1947.

Paapa Ossei's achievements cannot be mentioned without mentioning his very supportive and faithful wife, **Mrs Alexcia Adwoa Ossei**. Mrs Alexcia Ossei, formerly known as Alixcia Pat-Williams, was the daughter of an Aburi royal and a Trinidadian horticulturalist. Her father had been brought to Ghana from Trinidad and Tobago, in the Carribean, by the British colonial government. His assignment in Ghana was to help establish the **Aburi Botanical Gardens**. He ended up marrying a beautiful Aburi royal and spending the rest of his days in Ghana. **Mama Alexcia** had also trained as a teacher, at Wesley Girls High School in Cape Coast, and beautifully complemented her hardworking husband in his work. Mama taught for only a few years and had to start working from home, as the couple were blessed with more children.

Mama was an extraordinarily gifted seamstress, baker, fashion designer and women's ministry leader. She stood with her husband in the church, community, politics and philanthropy. When Paapa passed on, **Mama Alexcia** championed their joint ministry till she joined Paapa in eternity in 1993. She was a first in many things: She was the first female member of the St Georges Choir, the founder of Christian Mothers in Koforidua, the first Noble Lady of Ladies of Marshal in Koforidua, the designer of the first uniform for Madonna International School and the sole contractor to make the uniforms of Madonna school for the first few years. She was a leader given by God to **Paapa Ossei,** to support the work given to him. They were joined in Holy Matrimony at the first Catholic Church building in Koforidua, which was situated at the Catholic School complex where **Master Ossei** spent most of his working life. **Paapa's** pet name for Mama was, 'Alix' and Mama called Paapa, 'Mick'. They were two lovers on a heavenly mission.

Paapa's role as a church leader has been mentioned earlier, but there is more. As the first Catholics in Koforidua were from German Togoland, most of the Catholic services were done in the Ewe language from the beginning. **Sir Knight M. K. Ossei** was tasked with the responsibility of translating the Catholic Mass into the Twi language. A task he performed with distinction. He was an extraordinary interpreter, musician, playwright and concert producer. He formed the first St George's Catholic Choir, leading it as its first Choirmaster. He would teach the whole congregation to sing songs before the start of services.

He organised musicals and plays for the whole community. He translated the 15th century play 'Everyman' into the local Twi language musical, he titled "Odasani". He also produced the "Passion of Christ". These were free productions for the whole community performed in the local Twi language. They were so good that, the performers travelled to other cities within, and beyond the region, to perform. **Master Ossei** encouraged every class in the Catholic schools to have an end of year performance on stage, in front of the main twin tower Catholic Church building. Complex plays like 'Robin Hood' and 'Ali Baba and the Forty Thieves' have been performed at these festivals.

Sir Knight Michael Ossei was instrumental in organising the 1963 **'Golden Jubilee Celebration'** with the Rev Eindhoven. It was with great joy that Rev Eindhoven drove him from Nsawam Prison, where he had spent time as a political prisoner of the ruling CPP government, to continue his work in the community. The Catholic hierarchy had worked hard to secure his release as there was high political tension at the time.

Political History: The national assembly at that time had voted in 1962 to turn Ghana into a one-party state. This was a decision that would eventually become law in 1964. There had been a deterioration in relationship between the two main political parties: Convention People's Party (CPP) in government and United Party (UP) in opposition. After CPP won the 1956 election, they brought in a law: "Avoidance of Discrimination Act' which banned all parties which were considered regional or religious or sectarian. All the opposition parties were grouped under this. These parties therefore came together to form the United Party, under the leadership of Dr. Kofi Abrefa Busia. The parties in this alliance were: The Northern People's Party (NPP), National Liberation Movement (NLM), Muslim Association Party, Anlo Youth Organisation, Togoland Congress, Ga Shifimokpee.

'The Preventive Detention Act', which gave the CPP government the right to detain, without trial, anyone they considered dangerous, was passed in 1958. When Ghana became a republic in 1960, the official opposition was not recognised any more by the ruling government. **Paapa M. K. Ossei**, who had stood on the UP ticket and lost to the CPP candidate, in the previous election, became a target of arrest, and was detained under the 'Preventive Detention Act'. The Catholic Church pushed hard for him to be released after spending a time in detention. Some of his colleagues spent a longer time, and some even died there, like the leader of NLM, J. B. Danquah. Master Ossei's own good friend, Papa Yaw Boakye (M. M. Y Boateng) was only released after the CPP government was removed from office by the military in February 1966.

Coming back to his work with the church, **Master Ossei** was a master at organising local pageants which they called 'picnics' during which the church societies, in their colourful clothing, will dance through the streets, accompanied by brass band music to provide entertainment for the community and draw people to the Christian Faith. Both the old and young looked forward to these picnics. **Paapa** managed a dance band called 'The Rockies', who practised in the milk-bush fenced garden in the **Nana Pokua House** in Srodai and played at public events. Two of their remembered recordings were '**Ossei Nye/ Sw3 Sw3 Sw3 Akokc Sw3**.' Some of these bandsmen went on to become nationally recognised musicians playing in famous bands like Ramblers and Uhuru. **Master Ossei** was also one of the founders of Catholic Youth Organisation (CYO), aimed at building the young in the community to become responsible Christian adults.

In 1968, **Michael Kwasi Ossei was** elected to be Chairman of the Koforidua Municipal Council. In 1969, he was again chosen to represent Koforidua at the National Constituent Assembly, to draw a new constitution for Ghana. Later in 1969, he was elected as Member of Parliament to represent New Juaben constituency on the ticket of the Progress Party, led by Dr Kofi Abrefa Busia. He was appointed Deputy Minister at the Ministry of Information, and later at the Ministry of Works and Housing. Paapa served his church, community and nation to his fullest ability. His legacy is in the hearts of many, all over the world.

His biological children are Elizabeth Ossei, George Ossei, Anthony Ossei, Philomena Nortey, Irene Owusu Ansah, Augustina Awuraa Akosua Akoto, Michael Kwasi Ossei, Martin Kwadwo Ossei, Josephine Owusu and Patrick Yaw Ossei. Master exited this side of eternity to be with Jesus in February 1982.

CHAPTER 10

ABUSUAPANIN KWABENA OTI
(SIR KNIGHT PROF KWABENA BOAKYE-YIADOM)

Professor Kwabena Boakye Yiadom

Prof & Ante B

Prof the Academic

Prof with Asantehene Opoku Ware

Representing Ghana

Family Photo

Knight of St Sylvester

Young Prof with family

Professor **Kwabena Boakye-Yiadom** was Abusua Panin for the **Pokua-Ossei** family from 1982 to 2024. Like his uncle, M. K. Ossei, whom he succeeded as Abusua Panin in 1982, his leadership of the Abusua was exemplary. His leadership, like his predecessor, went beyond the family to affect many lives outside the family.

Prof Boakye Yiadom was born on 29th December 1938. He was christened **Augustine K. Boakye-Yiadom**. The Augustine disappeared over time, and he was generally called **Kwabena Boakye-Yiadom**. He had his early education at Koforidua Catholic Primary and Middle schools and moved on to Opoku Ware Catholic Secondary School in Kumasi. **Kwabena Ti**, as he was affectionately called, was an academically brilliant student, who continued the family tradition as an educator, rising to the highest levels of academia.

After his Secondary education, he was admitted to the University of Science and Technology (UST), now known as Kwame Nkrumah University of Science and Technology (KNUST), to study pharmacy. His brilliance earned him a scholarship to further his study in Europe. He returned from Europe with a doctorate degree (PHD), to teach at his old university in Kumasi.

While the Ossei legacy as educators and community leaders continued to bear fruit in Koforidua, **Dr Boakye-Yiadom** settled at UST, Kumasi, as a tributary of this great river flowing from Koforidua. His grandmother, **Nana Ama Pokua,** had made the great journey, 'Akwantu Kese', from Asante to Koforidua, New Juaben. A century later, **Dr Kwabena Boakye,** returned as an educator and influencer to Asante. He pursued his vocation with great enthusiasm. He rose to the height of his profession, before his retirement from active teaching in 1998.

The Asantehene, Otumfuo Opoku Ware II, and the Emeritus Archbishop Peter Akwasi Sarpong of Kumasi were his close friends and mentors.

As a senior lecturer at the University of Science and Technology, Kumasi, he obtained the prestigious Fulbright Scholarship, to do advanced study in Microbiology: "Screening herbal plants for antimicrobial agents" at the prestigious Howard University, USA in 1977. From the position of Senior Lecturer in the Pharmacy department of University of Science and Technology in 1969, **Dr Kwabena Boakye-Yiadom** was made 'Head of Department' in 1979. He became Dean of Faculty in 1983 and held the position of Pro Vice Chancellor of the university, from 1984 to 1988. He was a member of the University Council from 1992 to 1997.

He had fellowships in the regional pharmaceutical societies in Ghana and Wet Africa, bearing the letters 'FPSGH' and 'FWAPCP' in addition to his many qualifications and titles. **Professor Kwabena Boakye-Yiadom** was President of the Pharmaceutical Society of Ghana from 1989-1993. He was Chair of the Koforidua Technical University Council from 2001 to 2008. He served Koforidua in this capacity, even after his retirement from the University of Science and Technology.

It is interesting to note that **Professor Boakye-Yiadom's** maternal grandfather, **Agya Osei** (Nana Pokua's husband) was a notable herbalist. This probably had something to do with Prof's choice of profession. He was an educator as well as a medicine maker.

Professor Boakye Yiadom was known for his easy going, down to earth friendliness and sense of humour, a trait that runs through the Pokua-Ossei family. He was greatly loved by his family, students and peers alike, because of his hospitable and friendly nature. His self-deprecating humour, despite his many achievements, made others comfortable in his presence. It is said, he would leave his official car and driver, and squeeze himself unto overloaded public transport, just to be in solidarity and identify with the less privileged.

Like other members of the family, he played a central role in the Catholic church in Kumasi. The Boakye-Yiadom home was a second home to many young Catholic clergy, who were always welcome to his wise counsel and the beautiful cooking of Mama Beatrice, his wife. Many of the priests supported by Professor Boakye-Yiadom later served in high offices in the Catholic Church. Right Reverend Bishop John Opoku Agyeman of Konongo diocese and Vicar Generals, Monseigneurs Stephen Osei-Duah, Matthew Edusei and Louis Kofi Tuffour of the Kumasi archdiocese and Konongo diocese were all Professor Kwabena Boakye

Yiadom's mentees. Pope John Paul II recognised his services to the Catholic Church with the papal award of the **'Knight of St Sylvester'** which was bestowed on him in the year 2001.

As the adage goes, 'Behind every successful man is a great woman', **Professor Kwabena Boakye Yiadom** married the beautiful **Beatrice Frempong,** daughter of Maame Akua Korang (Madam Kate Boateng) in 1966. Beatrice comes from a well-established Koforidua Srodai family, and she also trained as a teacher. She was a great pillar of strength behind Prof for the nearly 60 years they were married. They got married when Professor Kwabena was doing his post-graduate studies in Europe. They were lovers till Professor Kwabena's passing in 2024. Her quiet, behind-the-scenes, organisation complemented the leadership gift of her husband.

This legacy of accomplishment has been passed on to their children: **Kwabena Oti Boakye-Yiadom**, **Kofi Boakye Yiadom**, **Nana Akua Boakye Yiadom**, **Acheampong Boakye-Yiadom**, **Lawrence Yaw Boakye-Yiadom, Kwadwo Boakye-Yiadom, Eno Adwoa Pokua Boakye-Yiadom**, and **Adwoa Agyemang Boakye-Yiadom**.

Thanks **Professor Sir Knight Kwabena Boakye-Yiadom**, for continuing the Pokua-Ossei legacy.

Professor Kwabena Boakye-Yiadom peacefully passed on to eternity in May 2024, while we were still putting this book together. **Rest well, Abusua Panin.**

CHAPTER 11
AKWADUM CHRISTIAN VILLAGE

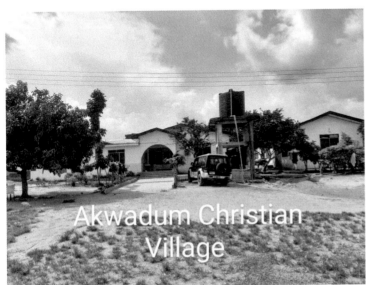

Akwadum Christian Village

Pastor Elizabeth Ossei

Mama Lizzie

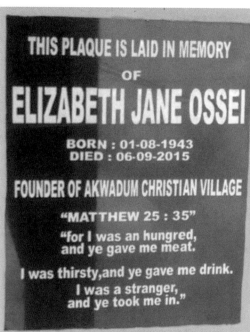

Classrooms

Akwadum school

Akwadum dormitory & buses

Children in worship

In class

Felicity

Children

Rev Greg & Mama Cecilia

Sister Lizzie & family

Akwadum Christian Village is one of the leading Orphanage and School complexes in the Eastern Region of Ghana. It is known for providing a place of refuge for orphans, trafficked and displaced children, particularly in the New Juaben district and surrounding areas. **The Akwadum Christian Village** was founded by **Reverend Elizabeth Akosua Ossei,** the first daughter of **Sir Knight M. K. Ossei**. This is part of the legacy of the Pokua-Ossei family.

The Akwadum Christian Village started its operations in Akwadum in 2006, but the vision had been birthed in the heart of **Mama Lizzie,** years earlier. God had given **Rev Elizabeth Ossei** a dream to build a village, that would cater for needy young children, old people, a clinic and a Church for the surrounding villages of Koforidua.

Akwadum was one of the settlement posts of the people of Juaben, when they migrated from Asante to settle in present-day Koforidua. When **Sister Elizabeth** got this vision from God, she immediately started laying the groundwork for the fulfilment of the vision.

After consultation with the leadership of **Christ Evangelical Church, London,** which she had founded in 1988, she went on to register a charity with the Charity Commission of England and Wales as she lived in England at the time. The working name of the charity is **Akwadum Christian Village**. The mission of the charity is listed as ***Education and Training, Prevention and Relief of Poverty, Oversees Aid and Famine Relief, Religious Activities, Recreation and Other Activities***.

The charity's aim is to provide helping hands services, advocacy, advice and information for Children and Young People, Elderly and Old People, People with Disabilities and the General Public.

Pastor Elizabeth Ossei approached the chief of Akwadum, **Odikro Nana Yaw Kyere,** to share her dream and ask for land to build the **Akwadum Christian Village**. Odikro Nana Yaw Kyere surprised **Mama Lizzie** by telling her that, God had given him a dream, prior to her arrival, that a woman was going to approach him, and God had shown the Odikro, the exact piece of land to offer her. He obeyed and offered the land to Mama Lizzie. This was a miracle, and a sign that God was in the project.

The sod for the project was cut in 1999, and construction work began. Two houses were built for the orphanage, and a third house was constructed for the old people's home. A school was built which, over the years, has grown to be a full-fledged primary and junior secondary school, serving a wide community of villages. Buses were bought to transport students from the remotest hamlets to enjoy the benefits of schooling. The campus has been further developed over the years.

The Pokua-Ossei family legacy of community service and building people, has continued to flow through the **Akwadum Christian Village**. The local department of Social Welfare makes use of the resource, by referring abandoned and orphan children to Akwadum Christian Village, to be taken care of. Behind this charitable assignment, is a strong vision to see the lives of people changed spiritually.

Evangelism, through the preaching of the gospel of the Lord Jesus Christ, has been a very important part of this assignment by **Pastor Liz.** The Pokua-Ossei Christian heritage has been the main motivation for all our charitable community work. This vision of evangelisation was realised with the support of **Christ Evangelical Church**, London, and a branch of the Church has been established at Akwadum. This assembly reaches out to the surrounding villages with the gospel of Jesus Christ. A branch of the Church has also been established at Okorase, Akwapim.

Reverend Elizabeth Akosua Pankye Ossei, the visionary, was born on 1st August 1943. After her initial education in Ghana, she obtained a scholarship to study Midwifery in Halifax, UK. She got to the peak of her nursing career, as a Senior Health Visitor in the National Health Service of the United Kingdom. She returned to work with the Ghana Health Service, from 1979 to 1981. She had a 'Damascus Road' experience (had a radical encounter with Jesus Christ like the Apostlle, Paul), and dedicated the rest of her life to the service of the Lord Jesus Christ. She founded the **Christ Evangelical Church** in Leytonstone London, with apostolic oversight of 'Voice of the Lord Ministries' in 1988. She relentlessly served the Lord in ministry and has produced many spiritual children, who themselves have become ministers of the gospel. She was a community leader both in the United Kingdom and Ghana. After an exemplary life and great service in the Lord's vineyard, **Sister Lizzie** went home to be with the Lord on 6th September 2015.

The vision of **Akwadum Christian Village** has continued and grown under the leadership of Rev Elizabeth's son, **Reverend Gregory Kwaku Korsah** and his wife, **Mrs Cecilia Korsah**. Elder **Alexander Kena Abrokwah,** of Christ Evangelical Church, London is the current Chair of Trustees of the **Akwadum Christian Village**. Mrs **Felicity Akosua Saheeb**, Pastor Elizabeth's daughter, oversees Publicity and Fund Raising. Volunteering teams have travelled from abroad to support this project. Politicians and other notable personalities have visited and given gifts.

The Pokua-Ossei family has taken this on board as a family project and supported with donations and celebrations. Some have celebrated their birthdays with the kids or given donations. What about celebrating your next birthday or anniversary with the kids, or donating to this charitable cause?

Let's publicise and support this vision, as we continue the legacy of our elders. **Long live Akwadum Christian Village.**

CHAPTER 12
KOFI'S STORY

Kofr & Dad

My name is **Michael Kofi Ossei**, a proud member of the Pokua-Ossei family. I have a good story to tell. I find it a privilege and honour to contribute to this family book. Yes, the name sounds familiar, as I was named after my grandfather, Sir Knight Michael Kwasi Ossei (Master Ossei). There are many Michaels and Mikes in our family, all of us named after this great man.

Our family has spread to many countries of the world. I represent the second generation of the family born abroad, outside our beloved Ghana. Infact, the Pokua-Ossei family in the United Kingdom has appointed me as the Mrantiehene (Chief of the young ones), a title I hope to live up to. I pray God will give me the wisdom to be a good example to the second generation diasporans in the UK.

I was born in Yorkshire, England, in a town called Huddersfield in 1976. My father is Anthony Kwasi Ossei, the second son of Master Ossei. My mother is Margaret Yeboah from Asiakwa. My probe into how I was born in Huddersfield, is always met with a smile and the short answer from my father of: "I was studying there". My mother is not that helpful either, as she will always direct me to ask my father. I am therefore resigned to being a Yorkshire boy, from the north of England.

My story takes an interesting turn as, at the age of 3 months, I was whisked from Huddersfield, England to Koforidua, Ghana. I was taken to live in the great house of my grandfather, **Master Ossei** and Grandma, **Mama Alexcia Ossei**. My earliest memory of the life in Koforidua was a house full of activity. I used to spend time in the same room as Grandad, and I vividly recall just watching him sit in his chair on the balcony of the big house, smoking his pipe. Grandma Alexcia was always active, organising people and things. I remember such freedom, running around the house into the kitchen and any other room of my choice. There was a friendly dog, running around and playing with me. My parents would visit with toys from the UK. I especially remember an aeroplane toy that would defy gravity, that lifted and went down. What a great time in the great house.

This haze of freedom and fun times were cut short after the passing of Grandad in the early part of 1982. The mood in the house changed. I recall his body being brought into the house, to be prepared for burial. Everyone was sad. Soon after, in the very same year, I was brought back to England, to Liverpool, also in the north of England, though not as northern as Huddersfield. I had to adapt to a new way of living: Cold weather, snow, endless rain and people speaking funny.

My time in Ghana, even as a 6-year-old, had made me fluent in Twi, our native language. Sadly, I have lost this fluency over the years and though I understand every word, I struggle to speak fluently. I am more fluent in English now, than my favourite Twi.

I am now married to the wonderful and beautiful Rosemary from the city of Benin in Nigeria, and God has blessed us with two lovely children: Matthew Anthony Ossei and Olivia-Marie Ossei.

When I look back to who I am today, I can see the contribution of family in every part of my life. I find it significant that I spent the last 6 years of my Grandad's life with him. He imparted something into my life. I have had very intimate times with my own dad too, that have impacted me. My uncles and aunties and cousins and nieces and family, have all contributed to who I am today. We are a close-knit family.

These experiences in life and support of family, drive me today. My children spend a lot of time with my daddy, **Anthony Ossei**, as I spent with his daddy, **Master Ossei**. He instils in them Ghanaian values, where I may fall short. Unfortunately, living in London, the chances of the kids being raised on ampesi, plantain and fufu are touch and go, as there will always be a plate of chips present. However, my father has had a profound impact on my children. My daughter likes fufu just like he does. She is also an avid reader, like my dad.

I hope my story attests to the fact that the Pokua-Ossei family lives on and is multiplying. I love my family, and I love Ghana. **Long live the Pokua-Ossei family**.

CHAPTER 13

BORN AND BRED IN J47

Kwabena & Faustina

I am **Emmanuel Kwabena Okyere Baffour**, a proud member of the esteemed Nana Pokua family from Srodai in Koforidua, Ghana's Eastern Regional capital. Raised with the guidance of my mother, **Madam Rosemary Frempong**, and my father, Kofi Akosomo, alongside my brother, Kwaku Boateng, I inherited a deep reverence for our cultural heritage and Catholic faith.

From a young age, I was immersed in the rich tapestry of Srodai's culture — the echoes of Catholic traditions, the bustling market scenes, and the stories of resilience passed down by my late grandmother, Nana Afia Boatemaa (aka Afia Enya, aka Cecilia Frempong), who raised twelve children, including my mother. Her strength and wisdom continue to guide me in both personal and professional endeavours.

Early on, I was drawn to the intricate web of connections that define both family ties and technological networks. This fascination led me to pursue a career in IT, specializing in networking — a field that resonates with the interconnectedness and reliability prized within our family.

In my professional journey, I strive to embody the principles of unity and resilience instilled by my ancestors. Networking, to me, is more than just configuring routers and switches. It is about building robust systems that enable seamless communication and collaboration, much like the strong bonds that tie the members of the Nana Pokua family together.

Along this journey, I found my soulmate in Faustina Baffoe, who hails from Senya in the Central Region of Ghana. Her laughter became the melody of my days, and together, we envision a future rooted in love, respect, and shared dreams. Our bond grew stronger amidst the mango trees of Srodae, where we nurtured our relationship with the same care that my grandmother had shown her twelve children.

Today, as I reflect on my path, I am grateful for the lessons of resilience and community instilled by my upbringing in Srodae. My faith in Jesus Christ has anchored me through life's challenges and celebrations, while my commitment to preserving our cultural heritage continues to shape my actions.

My story is one of embracing roots while reaching for new heights, guided by the values of family, faith, and love. In every step, from the dusty streets of Srodae to the broader horizons I've explored, I carry with me the strength of my ancestors and the enduring spirit of my community.

Emmanuel Kwabena Okyere Baffour
Koforidua Technical University

CHAPTER 14
SERVING MY NATION AS A SOLDIER

Captain Dionne

As the firstborn of Dr. Ralph Nyadu-Addo and Mrs. Adriana Nyadu-Addo, I, **Captain Dionne Nyadu-Addo**, am deeply proud of the rich family history that surrounds me in the Pokua-Ossei family. My upbringing was deeply intertwined with our heritage and Catholic faith, and although I primarily lived in Accra and Kumasi in my youth, Srodai remained a constant presence in my heart. **J47**, the **Pokua-Ossei** family home in Srodai, holds a special place in my heart, as it was here that Grandma **Philomena Comfort Boakye** played a pivotal role in shaping my life. I spent long periods of time with my lovely grandma. Her unwavering faith, strength, and wisdom continue to guide me, both personally and professionally.

Inspired by our esteemed family head, Prof. Boakye-Yiadom, I pursued my career in pharmacy and became a registered pharmacist in Ghana. However, another calling, a yearning to serve my nation, became known. The **Ghana Armed Forces** became my new home, and I currently hold the rank of Captain.

Everywhere I serve, I aim to elevate the name of Nana Pokua and solidify the bonds that connect our family. J47, the house that has witnessed generations of our family, feels even more significant to me because of this purpose. With every interaction and contribution, I make within these walls, I carry the values instilled by my family – faith, dedication, and pursuit of excellence.

The famous J47 may be a place within Srodai, but it represents much more. It is a tangible reminder of the Nana Pokua legacy, a source of unwavering support, and a constant call to serve the community.

Captain D. Nyadu-Addo
(Pharmacist, 37 Military Hospital)

CHAPTER 15
DR. ENO BOAKYE-YIADOM'S STORY

Dr Adwoa Pokua

My Name is **Eno Adwoa Pokua Boakye-Yiadom**. I am the fourth child of our departed Abusuapanin - **Prof Kwabena Boakye -Yiadom**. I am privileged to have been named after our great ancestor **Nana Pokua**. My Dad being an only son of Maame Panin, who was the daughter of Nana Pokua, he was pampered by his mum and his sisters. My early memory of **J47** house was my father bundling me and my siblings up during our primary school long holidays to Koforidua. His idea was for us not to lose our roots as we were born and bred fully in Kumasi. Our holidays in Koforidua were mostly with my maternal side but my dad would take us to see **Maame Panin** who would cook delicious meals for us. My few memories of J47 are all pleasant because of Maame Panin. The values of my famed great grandmother Nana Pokua which were passed on to my dad, I believe, have been passed on to us, his children.

I can easily see the values of emotional strength and maturity, resilience in the face of adversity, hardworking and leadership and the fear of God in me and my siblings. This is what has made me who I am today: A Pastor, Doctor and a mother. Of course, I cannot disregard the mighty Grace of God as I agree and join Paul in proclaiming that, *"I am what I am by the Grace of God"*. (1 Corinthians 15 vs 10).

My prayer is that we all will pass these great attributes and values of our cherished family to the next generation as they carry on the torch of our Great grandmother **Nana Pokua**.

Dr Adwoa Pokua Boakye-Yiadom
Okomfo Anokye Teaching Hospital, Kumasi

CHAPTER 16
A WORD FROM DR JOSEPHINE OWUSU (NEE OSSEI), ONTARIO, CANADA

Osei Owusu Photography

Dr Josie Owusu

Knowing we cannot choose our family as humans, makes belonging to ours, a win-win situation, and a blessing. It is not a perfect family by any means, but the zeal to remain inclusive, helpful and engaged in activities that honor our predecessors, parents, our children and ourselves, is what will keep the essence of the Pokua-Ossei family continually glowing.

Growing up, I remember our gathering at J47 on Christmas mornings to pray and celebrate. One could not miss or be late for this. It was an event we all enjoyed thoroughly, but also took for granted. Little did I know at the time, that Paapa Master Ossei was instilling togetherness amongst us. We all left feeling joyful and ready to dig into our akokɔ nkwaen (chicken soup) and fufuo later in the day. Maame Yaa was always the gracious matron, hosting all of us, and evidently proud of her brother. Uncle John Frempong was the unofficial family secretary and ɔkyeame (linguist).

Paapa was Master Ossei, community leader, minister of state and all, but to us, he was just a loving dad. I remember when he made Christmas hats from colourful construction paper and tinsels. One of the fundamental legacies he left was his strong, pragmatic faith. Mama Alexcia Ossei was industrious, nurturing and fiercely practical in her faith as well. I recall the long walks from Asaasim, our home on Accra Road, to St George's Church for the Monday evening charismatic prayer meetings.

I believe we are reaping the results of their good work and the foundations they laid. What is impressive though, is the new emerging drive to energize, unify and lift the family. May the Good Lord guide this mission and bless us all in our respective endeavors. In God we trust.

Josephine Afua Akyeampomaa Owusu (Sista)

CHAPTER 17
SPECIAL TRIBUTES

This page is dedicated to young family members who passed on to eternity in the recent past. *"You went too soon, but God knows best. We miss you, but we are consoled that you are in a better place, with our Father in heaven"*.

MRS BRIDGET SHEVON MENDS AMPEM (Ama Sweety) was born to Philomena Boakye (Yaa Asatewa) of the Pokua-Ossei family and Mr Mends, a hotelier and entrepreneur from Cape Coast. She was born in Koforidua on 3rd March 1962. She was Yaa Asantewa's second child, after Olive Sheila Mends (Maame Efua). The former Vicar General of the Accra archdiocese, Very Reverend Francis Adoboli was one of Ama's classmates at the Koforidua Catholic Primary School. She furthered her education at the Koforidua New Juaben Secondary School, continuing at Apam Secondary School. The 'Ama Sweety' name of **Bridget Mends Ampem** was because she was very pretty and dressed fashionably, even as a child. Her contagious smile, and pleasant nature earned her the name, **Ama Sweetie**. Ama went into business after school, taking after her grandmother, Yaa Takyiaw, and father, Mends. She started as a clearing agent at Kotoka International Airport (AFGO Village), and then established a fashion shop which sold clothing, shoes and cosmetics near the 37 Military Hospital in Accra. **Ama Sweety** left us for heaven on Valentine's Day (14th February) 2005, during childbirth, a few days short of her 43rd birthday. Ama was in hospital to give birth to her first daughter. She already had 3 sons: Anthony (Tony), Raphael (Edem) and Emmanuel (Nana Yaw). Ama and her baby daughter did not make it back from the hospital. God knows best. Emmanuel Mensah, our New York hero soldier was Ama Sweety's son. **We will remember you, Ama Sweety. God knows best.**

JULIET POKUAH BAMPOE ANTWI (Julie/ JOBA) was born on 4th July,1962 at Anyinam to Mrs. Veronica Reinduls Bampoe and Mr. Charles Bampoe, all of blessed memory. Both parents were teachers by profession. Juliet had her basic education in Nkawkaw and studied fashion design at Mancell Vocational Institute in Kumasi.

She started her own fashion design shop in Nkawkaw where she lived with her late dad. During that time, Teacher Bampoe, her father, would send her to check up on his motor bike at Tomos Gh. LTD. On one of such rounds, she met Rev. George Antwi (former Head Pastor, Living Hope Baptist Church, Kumasi) who at that time was the workshop supervisor at Tomos Gh. LTD.

They got married after a period of dating and Juliet relocated to stadium, a suburb in Kumasi from Nkawkaw. She continued her fashion business in Kumasi, and it grew to become one of the top fashion centres in Kumasi. Her fashion centre was called JOBA.

Juliet and her husband had a son, Patrick Antwi Acheampong (Kofi Acheampong). Juliet was a devoted Christian, a Catholic by birth and a Baptist by marriage. She was a lively woman and full of hope and aspirations for the future, she loved to help people and would share what she had with others. She demonstrated her strong faith practically. Juliet left us to join her Creator in 2007, at the age of 45years, after a short illness. There are so many memories of Juliet, and the family wished she had lived for much longer, but the Lord knows best. **Rest well JOBA, forever in our hearts.**

REVEREND FATHER SAMUEL OWUSU FREMPONG: Father Samuel Owusu Frempong was the first ordained Catholic Priest of the Pokua-Ossei family. He was the great grandson of Nana Pokua. He was born on 25th August 1962 to Kwasi Antumi's son, Kwasi Duah (Anthony Kwasi Owusu) and Grace Adarkwa of Sorodai. He attended Pope John Minor Seminary and St Peter's Major Seminary and was ordained into the priesthood in July 1992. He was known for his fiery preaching and deep spirituality. He was the Mass Serving secretary at St Georges Catholic Church in his youth and was highly commended for his dedication to duty. He was the Seminary Prefect during his days at Pope John's Minor Seminary. He worked at Asamankese, Nkawkaw and Anyinam Catholic Churches after his ordination. He was appointed the first Youth Chaplain of the newly created Koforidua diocese of the Catholic Church. His bishop, Rt Rev Palmer Buckle, commended him as one of his best and most dedicated priests. He was alive to officiate at the funerals of his grandmothers, Akosua Abon and Yaa Takyiaw, as well as the funeral of his father, Kwasi Duah. He passed on to be with his Lord on 31st May 2001. **We will remember you, Father Samuel. God knows best.**

PATRICK WILLIAM YAW OSSEI (Broda) Patrick was the last-born child of Abusuapanin, Sir Knight Michael Ossei (Master Ossei) and Mrs Alexcia Ossei. He was born on 6th September 1962. He was fondly named after his maternal grandfather, Joseph Adolphus Pat-Williams from Trinidad, but everyone called him Broda. He was the darling of the family, and everyone's favourite little brother. His handsome looks and carefree happy-go-lucky nature made him the soul of any party. He was one of the pioneer pupils of Madonna School, following on to St Peter's Secondary School, Nkwatia, finishing his sixth form at Pope John Sec School, Koforidua. The students at Pope John's Secondary School overwhelmingly chose him as their entertainment prefect for his outgoing nature and his musical ability. He was a good bass guitar player. He gained admission to study Public Administration at the University of Ghana, Legon. He travelled to the United Kingdom, seeking greener pastures. On his return from the United Kingdom, our delightful brother was taken from us in the prime of his life. **We will remember you, Patrick. God knows best.**

Hilary Kwame Asiedu

HILARY KWAME OSEI POKU ASIEDU (Hilly) Hilly was born on September 13, 1969, to Akua Ago (Joana Boakye) and Kofi Yamoah Asiedu from Trabuom, and of the Bantama Anoo stool of Asante. Hilly was always full of life and energy, and his presence generated enthusiasm. He was made the school prefect at Kwaku Boateng Experimental School. He would enthusiastically have a go at anything that was doable. There was a boldness about him that was admirable. Even when, in his primary school days, he was put in goal against Sarkodie Memorial School in a soccer match, and conceded 3 easy goals, Hilly was able to turn it into a humorous historical event. Everyone remembers when Hilly conceded 3 goals. He had his secondary school education at Pope John's Secondary School, Koforidua. He was an enthusiastic people's person. He was the popular leader of the Junior Auxiliary (Junior group of the Knights of Marshall) at St Georges Catholic Church. He was referred to as the "Family Soldier". You do not mess with Hilly's family. You mess with his family, you mess with Hilly, and he was a fearless fighter. Hilly was an accomplished videographer and was the video man of choice for many events in Koforidua, including royal events. Hilly left us for his home in heaven on May 8, 2003. His children are Hilary Fiifi Asiedu and Maame Yaa. **We will remember you, Hilly. God knows best.**

Nii Nortei Nortey

NII NORTEI NORTEY Nortei was the first-born son of Victor Okwei Nortey and Philomena Nortey. He was also the grandson of Abusua Panin Sir Knight M. K. Ossei. He was born on 14th October 1972. He had his primary education at University Primary School, Legon, and his Secondary at Achimota School, Accra. He then travelled to the United Kingdom where he pursued his love for computing and business. On returning from the United Kingdom, he helped to establish the computing department of Salem Secondary School and set up a tourism business: 'Ninns Ventures'. Though he was passionate about business, his greatest legacy was his compassionate support for the vulnerable. His life on this earth was cut short in 2023 after a short illness. At his funeral, there was a lot of tears, as many testified of how Nortei had rescued them from homelessness to give them hope. Some people testified that they lived with Nortei in his flat, rent free, for several months before they found their feet to move on. Nii Nortei was a generous and compassionate soul who cared for people. This was reflected in the good number of people, including several from the 'ghetto', who turned up at his funeral. When his old school mates gathered around his coffin to sing an anthem for him, there was not a dry eye in the packed Legon Catholic Church. **We will remember you, Nii Nortei Nortey. God knows best.**

PRIVATE FIRST-CLASS EMMANUEL MENSAH: Emmanuel is a decorated American soldier, who also happens to be the great, great grandson of Nana Ama Pokua. Private Emmanuel's death was mourned all over the world, as he lost his life in an act of great heroism. He saved 4 lives from an apartment building on fire in New York, U.S.A. In this selfless heroism, he lost his own life. 12 people were consumed by this raging fire. This was the deadliest fire in New York City in at least a quarter of a century. Private Mensah's heroism was on the lips of the whole world when this happened on 28th December 2017. Among many citations, he received the 2 highest posthumous medals from the United States Army for this act of bravery: **The Soldier's Medal** (The US army's top award for valour outside of combat) and **New York State Medal for Valour** (The State of New York highest military award). Emmanuel's funeral service was officiated by His Eminence Cardinal Timothy Dolan, Catholic Archbishop of New York Archdiocese, as a special honour for his bravery. A street has been named after him in Bronx, New York: **Private First-Class Emmanuel Mensah Way.** Emmanuel was the son of Kwabena O Mensah and Brigitte Ama Mends, daughter of Yaa Asantewa (Philomena Boakye). Emmanuel was born on 11th April 1991. The family emigrated to the US and Emmanuel enlisted in the New York Army National guard. Pfc Emmanuel Mensah, the Pokua-Ossei family is proud of you. **We will remember you, Emmanuel. God knows best.**

CHAPTER 18
WORDS OF WISDOM FROM LIVING ELDERS

OPANIN JOSEPH KOFI ADARKWA-YIADOM

God has put us together as a family. My little advice is that we should love one another and walk together as a family. Let us be there for one another in times of need and celebrate with each other when it calls for celebration. Let the world see us as a good example of how a family should be. Let us also not forget to pray for one another. God bless us all.

MADAM JOANA BOAKYE (Obaa Panin Akua Ago)

Being part of big family was gratifying. The elderly ensured food was available. Awo Akyaa would usually bring palm nuts from the farm; prepared the delicious "afabaawom" (pot-mix), which everyone was welcome to enjoy. Most families in the neighbourhood envied this family bonding.

The entire family is very active in church. I remember Mrs. Alexcia Ossei would organize us as members of the Christian Mothers, for comedy, concerts, and artistic performances to raise funds for the Christian Mothers. We toured several towns in the Eastern Region doing several shows in Tafo and Nkawkaw. I personally travelled to Accra on several occasions to raise funds for the Church's annual harvest. I was also the Choir Mother for the St. George's Church Choir for many years.

The family placed great value on education. For instance, I was very excited to be one of the few students to pass the common entrance examination when it was first introduced. I was in middle school form two at the time.

I have had great support from my children and family. I especially want to mention my daughter, Phiona, who has been my close companion, caring for me in my old age. God has blessed me to be 81 years on earth so far. I take my medical check-ups seriously. I can still sing and dance to praise the Lord. I am careful to eat healthily. I would advise the young ones: Do not get sucked by superstitious beliefs. Take good care of yourself. Seek peace. It is better to politely pull people on the side to peacefully address your differences. Sometimes you realize the person you have issues with meant no harm.

MR ANTHONY KWASI OSSEI

I appreciate the writing of a book like this. Not only does it give the history of our family, but it also helps to bring the family together. We used to be the young ones in the family, but now we have become the elders. Our children have become adults and are giving birth to their own children. The family continues to grow.

Let's make God our number one in everything we do. The good book tells us that we reap what we sow. Let us sow love and good, wherever we are. We thank God for the unity and cooperation in the family. Long may it continue. As our children know our history and story, they will never forget their roots wherever they are in the world. I pray for God's blessing on our family.

MRS MARGARET AKOSUA BANNOR

I look back with great joy to the times when we were young and growing up in the great Pokua household. There was such love and oneness in the house that you would not know which children belonged to which mother. Every mother cooked for all the children and on special occasions like Christmas, we the children did not only receive gifts from our own parents. Everyone gave generously to everyone. I will encourage the young ones today to learn from the strong family bond in those days. You would not even notice the difference between family and tenants in the house. Everyone was treated as family. Everyone shared.

In our present self-centred world, my prayer is that we would go back to serve God well and love our family and neighbours as ourselves. Long live the Pokua-Ossei family.

MADAM ANNA FREMPONG

One thing that I have always cherished in my heart is the love and togetherness we had as children of different mothers living together in the Pokua household. We ate together and did everything as one family. Of course, times have changed. We have multiplied in number, and we are not all living in one house. Let us not forget that we are one family. Let us continue to love one another and walk in unity.

I ask that the Lord heals everyone in the family, especially the elderly. There are many elderly in the family now and I am one of them. The younger ones must not forget to pray for and support the elderly. I pray that the young ones would have jobs and good families to live good lives. Our family has been built on the foundation of Christ. I pray that the young ones would not abandon their faith and those who have left the faith will come back.

MADAM MARY BANAHENE (Obaa Panin Serwaa Barnie)

The family was closely knit. I remember Sister Anna, Sister Philo, Sister Irene, and I, will bring food from our mothers' pots and we will sit together and enjoy our meals together. It was more fun to eat together.

I admired Awo Afia Nyame greatly. She made sure food was always available in the house in the city, though she spent most of her time on the farms in the village. She would load food in baskets ready for us to carry home from the farm. All we had to do was, just go to the village and bring it home. There are times Awo Afia Nyame will carry the food stuff halfway to meet us. Awo Afia Nyame would carry food to us, on her way to church, on Sundays. Education was very important for the family. Monday through Thursday was study days. Fun day was Fridays.

I would counsel that, as a family, we love each other and live together as one beautiful people, as it has always been. I would like to remind all of us, to adjust our lifestyle to healthy living.

MRS PHILOMENA AMA NORTEY

I am honoured to be part of this great family. We are a big family, and though we are all unique according to how God has made us, God himself put us in the Pokua-Ossei family. It is a good privilege that the bible tells us that if we invite God, He will gladly come and live in us. We must all invite Him. If we do, then He who lives in us is greater than he who is in the world (1 John 4:4). My prayer is that everyone of us will have a close relationship with Jesus Christ. One of the great strengths of our family is that it has been built on the foundation of Christ. We must live in this legacy of our parents and make Jesus Christ the foundation of everything we do.

When we were young and we all lived in the old Pokua family home, there was such love that we did everything together and it was lovely. When every mother cooked, it was for everyone. Children from the same age group, from the different mothers would eat together from the same bowl. My prayer is that the love that existed then would continue in our hearts for one another, for God is love. One person's child becomes our child, and we support each other to be a blessing to the whole family.

My prayer is that even as our numbers increase, let us hold fast to our faith in the midst of the many distractions of the world. We must pray for one another and encourage each other to greater faith. God bless us all as a family.

MADAM BEA MENSAH (Sister Abena K11)

I am happy that a history of our great family is being put together. As the family has grown larger, we have grown more apart. When we were younger, we used to do everything together as a family and it was fun. There were no brick wall separating J47 from K11. I especially remember when we would have great parties every 26th December (boxing day), when every mother would bring food and drinks, and we would have a big Christmas party together. My prayer is that our children and grandchildren will know one another and be there for each other as one family. God bless us all.

MADAM AUGUSTINA AKOTO (AWURAA AKOSUA)

I am so glad that our family is getting together through this book. Because of work and travel, our children do not know each other as they should. There is a time for everything, and I thank God that this can bring us together. My prayer is that we will all walk in love and godliness as our parents taught us. Let us be a family of prayer and support each other. God bless you all.

MRS IRENE OWUSU-ANSAH (nee Ossei) Afua Boatemaa

The Nana Pokuaah family of Koforidua, New Juaben, is truly blessed. We are blessed with a historical tableau of calm, social, spiritual. and academic achievers with superb but self-effacing leadership skills. Skills that have run through the generations, from the matriarch, Nana Ama Pokuaah, from the time of the great journey From Old Juaben, 150 years ago, through her offspring, to the present, in the 21st century.

Over the years, the family has remained strongly bonded to each other, and to Koforidua Ghana. Although various members have spread their wings to other parts of Ghana, and many others journeyed to different parts of the world including, The United Kingdom, United States, Canada, and Italy, the family bonds remain, crossing several generations and age differences.

As the matriarch of those of us in the diaspora, the 5th child of Master Ossei, I appreciate the worth and contribution of every member of this wonderful family and am committed to continuing to foster and strengthen the family bonds that exist between us. We are each comfortable, strong, and independent, but TOGETHER we can be stronger. A formidable God-fearing force. An example of how a family should be. A beacon for other extended families to emulate.

May the Lord Continue to bless each member of this family.

MADAM ROSEMARY FREMPONG

I am glad to be part of this strong and loving family. My little bit of prayer and counsel is that we would continue to love each other as a family and love others. I pray that we would continue to serve God and serve others. When we humble ourselves, God will bless us. Thank you.

MR ANTHONY OWUSU (On behalf of Kwasi Antumi's grandchildren)

We the grandchildren of Opanin Kwasi Antumi are very proud to be members of this noble family. Even though we were not fortunate to know our grandfather, his siblings, nephews, and nieces have consistently demonstrated true love for our grandmother Akosua Abon, mother, Grace Adarkwa and us. From a tender age we were made to know that our grandfather came from this family.

Sir Knight Michael Ossei who inherited our grandfather, contributed a lot to the upbringing of our father, Kwasi Duah and his children. Master ensured that we gained admission to the Catholic Primary School without any stress, and he monitored our education and behaviour. He gave our grandmother the opportunity to provide meals for the pupils in the school, to enable her to earn some income to take care of us. Grandma Auntie Alexcia always showed us love and called us grandchildren.

George Ossei was very close to our father, Kwasi Duah, and was a father to us. All our other aunties and uncles were very cordial and welcoming to us.

Grandma Takyiaw and our grandma, Akosua Abon, were very close friends. She and her children were very kind and supportive to us and contributed a lot to our upbringing. The Frempongs were also kind to us and continue to acknowledge us as siblings. Even though our grandfather died early, we were not left on our own.

I can write a whole book about the positive experiences we gained from this family. It is indeed a loving, disciplined and Christian family that showed love to all that they encountered. No wonder the Ossei family and the Asante family played a great and positive role in the growth of the Catholic Church in Koforidua. It is our prayer that we continue to strengthen this bond of love and brotherhood.

Long live the Pokua and Ossei family. May the Good Lord continue to pour His blessings on all its members. Shalom.

REVEREND MICHAEL KWASI OSSEI

I love my family. I pray God will help me to do more to help promote the better development of the great Pokuaa - Ossei family. The family has always been one of the centre points in my life.

My parents, Master Ossei and Madam Alexcia, were very particular in the way they helped to form the relationships my siblings and I now have. They understood that life is much easier to have people that are there for you and care about you. That is family.

Through the beautiful experience I have had with my family, I understand why our parents raised us as a close family. I believe in family unity as one of the most important aspects of life. This should be central in the way we raise family.

We are like a little Church. Establishing a common philosophy and goals can help unite the family in ways you never expected. The child you thought was the most difficult may rise and take the lead. A longstanding grudge between you and a family member could melt away as you make the effort to love and cherish family unity.

As Pope Francis mentioned in one of his homilies on the family: "God blesses every step we take because he is so committed to family life. He loves watching us become shining lights of love and unity in this world."

I love my wife, Alexandra, 3 daughters Alexcia, Michelle, Jennifer and my 2 grandchildren, Phoebe and Tessa. I love my entire extended family, and my prayer is that our family will be committed to family unity.

ABUSUAPANIN WILLIAM YAW BRIGHT ASARE

I count it a blessing to be part of this great Pokua-Ossei family. I am honoured to have been chosen as the Abusua Panin to succeed my uncle Professor Kwabena Boakye Yiadom when he passed on to heaven. My prayer is that God will give me the wisdom and strength to undertake this big responsibility. I am confident that with the help and support of everyone in our family, we will continue to grow and contribute our part for a better world.

My prayer is that the family would continue to support one another. Our love for God should grow, and I want to see more ministers of the gospel of Jesus Christ produced in the family. Our family has always made education important. This must continue. Let us continue to support each other to higher heights. God bless us all.

Boatemaa Bannor

CHAPTER 20
FAMILY DIRECTORY

A

1. Abd-Allah Adwoa Agyeiwaa (Mrs), **Tema, Ghana**
2. Abena Akyaa (D)
3. Abrokwah James Nana, **Ghana**
4. Acheampong Kwaku, **Ghana**
5. Acquaah Gina, **London, UK**
6. Adarkwah Yiadom Kofi **London UK**
7. Adarkwah Jennifer Abena Boatemaa **Canada**
8. Addo Alicia Asantewaa, **Ghana**
9. Addo Anita, **Ghana**
10. Addo Audrey Kokwe, **Ghana**
11. Addo Augustus Nana, **Kumasi, Ghana**
12. Addo Joe, **Ghana**
13. Addo Kwarteng
14. Addo Rita, **Ghana**
15. Addo Samuel Kofi, (D)
16. Addo William Annor, **Ghana**
17. **Afia Sakra, (D)**
18. Afrakomaa Sarah Akua, **London, UK**
19. Afriyie Ama, **Ghana**
20. Agboli Anthony, **Accra, Ghana**
21. Agboli Ralph Edem, **Accra, Ghana**
22. Aidoo Yvonne (D)
23. Akoto Awuraa Akosua Augustina, **Koforidua, Ghana**
24. Akyaa Abena Awo, (D)
25. Akyamah Lydia, **Ghana**
26. Allotey Charles, **Koforidua,Ghana**
27. Allotey Jeff Aquaye, **Koforidua, Ghana**
28. Allotey Jude, **Koforidua, Ghana**
29. Allotey Kingsley, **Koforidua, Ghana**
30. Allotey Perry, **Koforidua, Ghana**
31. Amoah Comfort (Bobosey), **(D)**
32. Amoah Comfort Yaa Boatemaa, **Ghana**
33. Amoah Godfried Kwadwo Panin, **Ghana**
34. Amoah Edmond **London, UK**
35. Amoah Edna Nhyira **London, UK**
36. Amoah Eugene Kwabena **(D)**
37. Amoah Gyekye Alexcia (Mrs), **Halifax, Canada**
38. Amoah Gyekye John (Pastor), **Halifax, Canada**
39. Amoah Gyekye Joshua, **Halifax, Canada**
40. Amoah Gyekye Nathan, **Halifax, Canada**
41. Amoah Jerome, (**London, UK**)
42. Amoah Joyce Panin, **Ghana**
43. Amofa Emmanuel Kofi, **Koforidua, Ghana**
44. Anim-Ofosuhene Adom Kwaku, **Ghana**
45. Anomah Felicia, **Nkawkaw, Ghana**
46. Anomah Gloria, **Nkawkaw, Ghana**
47. Anomah Veronica, **Nkawkaw, Ghana**
48. Ansah Augusata Abena Adowa (D)
49. Ansah Elise Boatemaa **Maryland, USA**
50. Ansah Evan Xavier **Maryland USA**
51. Ansah Joanna (Mrs), **Maryland, USA**
52. Anthonio Bellina, **Canada**
53. Anthonio Brenda, **Canada**
54. Anthonio Chrysanthus, **Accra, Ghana**
55. Anthonio Kelvin, **USA**
56. Anthonio Keziah, **Canada**
57. Anthonio Linda Awo Sika Bannor (Mrs) **Accra, Ghana**
58. **Antumi Kwasi (Nana) (D)**
59. Antwi Ethanah Pokua, **Kumasi, Ghana**
60. Antwi Jeremiah George, **Kumasi, Ghana**
61. Antwi Juliet Bampoe Pokua (Mrs) (D)
62. Antwi Patrick Achaempong, **Kumasi, Ghana**
63. Anyimadu Ama Pokua (Mrs), **Koforidua, Ghana**
64. Apau Kwadwo, **London, UK**

65. Aryeh Zuriel Odoi, **Ghana**
66. Asamoah Charles, **Koforidua, Ghana**
67. Asante Akosua, **Ghana**
68. Asante Angelyn Nana Bannor (Mrs), **USA**
69. Asante Belinda, **Ghana**
70. Asante Charles, **Ghana**
71. Asante David, **USA**
72. Asante Eddie, **Ghana**
73. Asante Elias **(D)**
74. Asante Emma, **USA**
75. Asante Emmanuel, **USA**
76. Asante Jacqueline, **Ghana**
77. Asante Kwabena Owusu, **Akim Tafo, Ghana**
78. Asante Morgan **(D)**
79. Asante Paul, **Ghana**
80. Asante Pearl, **Ghana**
81. Asante Priscilla Kwaatemaa, **Ghana**
82. Asante Ruby, **Ghana**
83. Asante Sampson Atta, **Ghana**
84. Asantewaa Yaa, **Ghana**
85. Asiama Yaw, **USA**
86. Asiedu Adrian Marcus, **USA**
87. Asiedu Damian Asante, **USA**
88. Asiedu Hillary (Hilly) **(D)**
89. Asiedu Hillary Fiifi (Ghana)
90. Asiedu Felix Kwabena, **USA**
91. Asiedu Phiona, **Accra, Ghana**
92. Aso Afua, **Ghana**
93. Ayanleke Bade, **UK**
94. Ayanleke Michelle Ossei (Dr) **UK**
95. Ayanleke Tessa Tantaluwa, **UK**
96. Awura Akosua **(D)**

B

1. Baffoe David Nana Afrane, **London, UK**
2. Baffoe Faustina, **Koforidua, Ghana**
3. Banahene Mary Barnie, **Koforidua, Ghana**
4. Bannor Ben Kwabena, **London, UK**
5. Bannor Benita, **London, UK**
6. Bannor Bennard, **London, UK**
7. Bannor Catherine Boatemaa, **London, UK**
8. Bannor Daniel, **London, UK**
9. Bannor Daryl, **London, UK**
10. Bannor Denzel, **London, UK**
11. Bannor Ellen, **London, UK**
12. Bannor Emma, **London, UK**
13. Bannor George Yaw, **London, UK**
14. Bannor Hannah, **London, UK**
15. Bannor Jemimah, **Accra, Ghana**
16. Bannor Margaret Akosua, **Accra, Ghana**
17. Bannor Reginald Kwasi, **London, UK**
18. Boadi Asiedu Comfort Danso, **(D)**
19. Boahemaa Akosua **(D)**
20. Boahemaa Audrey, **Ghana**
21. Boahene Charlotte, **Accra, Ghana**
22. Boahene Claudia, **Accra, Ghana**
23. Boahene Esta, **Accra, Ghana**
24. Boahene Jude, **Koforidua, Ghana**
25. Boahene Jude, **Accra, Ghana**
26. Boahene Judy, **Accra, Ghana**
27. Boafo Kwaku Jnr, **Ghana**
28. Boakye Ariella, **Canada**
29. Boakye Brittany, **Canada**
30. Boakye Cassandra, **Canada**
31. Boakye Derrick Antwi, **Ghana**
32. Boakye Emmanuel Joloni, **Canada**
33. Boakye Emmanuel Kofi, **Canada**
34. Boakye Joanna Akua, **Accra, Ghana**
35. Boakye Kingsley Sarpong, **Accra, Ghana**
36. Boakye Leonard Dela, **Canada**
37. Boakye Philomena A, **Ghana**
38. Boakye Philomena Yaa **(D)**
39. Boakye Stephen Abrokwah, **Ghana**
40. Boakye-Yiadom Acheampong, **Kumasi, Ghana**
41. Boakye-Yiadom Adwoa, **USA**
42. Boakye-Yiadom Awo Brempomaa, **Ghana**
43. Boakye-Yiadom Ayeyi Papa Oti, **Kumasi, Ghana**

44. Boakye-Yiadom Beatrice, **Ghana Papa Oti**
45. Boakye-Yiadom Eno Pokua, **Kumasi, Ghana**
46. Boakye-Yiadom Felicia, **Ghana**
47. **Boakye-Yiadom Kwabena Oti (Prof) (D)**
48. Boakye-Yiadom Kwadwo, **Ghana**
49. Boakye -Yiadom Lawrence, **USA**
50. Boakye-Yiadom Nana Akua, **London, UK**
51. Boakye-Yiadom Nhyira Frempomaa, **Kumasi, Ghana**
52. Boakye-Yiadom Oti, **Tema, Ghana**
53. Boakye-Yiadom Oti Kofi, **Teme, Ghana**
54. Boatemaa Ama, **Suhum, Ghana**
55. Boatemaa Janet Ama, **Ghana**
56. Boateng Jude Nana Kwame, **Ghana**
57. Boateng Kingsley Nana Kwasi, **Ghana**
58. Boateng Kwaku, **Ghana**
59. Boateng Kwasi Okyenasco, **(D)**
60. Boateng Rita Nana Ama, **Ghana**
61. Brainoo Jennifer Ossei, **Slough, UK**
62. Brainoo Phoebe Oduma, **Slough, UK**
63. Brainoo Samuel, **Slough, UK**
64. Bright Asare Edward (D)
65. **Brenya Afia (Maame Anya), (D)**
66. Bright Asare Louis, **Tema, Ghana**
67. Bright Asare Nana Ntiwa, **Tema, Ghana**
68. Bright Asare Olivia, **Koforidua, Ghana**
69. Bright-Asare Samuel, **Tema, Ghana**
70. Bright-Asare William Yaw, **Tema, Ghana**

C

1. Commodore Michael Jnr, **Ghana**
2. Commodore Michael, **Ghana**

D

1. Darko Abena, **USA**
2. Darko Akua, **USA**
3. Darko Kofi, **USA**
4. Dei Akosua, **Ghana**

5. Duah Aaron Nana. **Takoradi, Ghana**

F

1. Fosu Kwabena, **(D)**
2. Frempong Adwoa Pokua Georgina, **Koforidua, Ghana**
3. Frempong Akua Duku Mansah (D)
4. Frempong Anna Akua, **Koforidua, Ghana**
5. Frempong Ante Ataa (Mrs), **Koforidua, Ghana**
6. Frempong Catherine Badu, **Koforidua**
7. Frempong John Maxwell (D)
8. Frempong Martin Kwadwo (D)
9. Frempong Monica, **Koforidua, Ghana**
10. Frempong Rita, **USA**
11. Frempong Rosemary Abena, **Koforidua, Ghana**
12. Frempong Yaw Manu (D)
13. Frimpong Gordon Yaw, **(D)**
14. Fye Layla, **London, UK**

H

1. Hansen Jacqueline Nana Yaa, **Ghana**
2. Hinson Ama Miriam Ampaabeng, **Ghana**
3. Hinson Candy Kwansimaa, **Ghana**
4. Hinson Edward Kwaku, **Koforidua, Ghana**

K

1. Keddy Kwame, **Canada**
2. Keddy Yaw Mensah, **Canada**
3. Kissiwaa Yaa, **Koforidua, Ghana**
4. Koboa, **Ghana**
5. Konadu Maame Adwoa, **Ghana**
6. Korang Abena (D)
7. Korang Yaa, **(D)**
8. Korsah Cecilia (Mrs), **London,UK**
9. Korsah Elizabeth Maafia, **London, UK**
10. Korsah Gregory Kwaku (Rev), **London, UK**
11. Korsah Henry, **London, UK**

M

1. **Maa Abena (D)**
2. **Maama Paulo (D)**
3. Marfo Bless Nana Akua, **USA**
4. Marfo Florence Achiaa, **Kumasi, Ghana**
5. Mark Kwadwo Ketewa, **Ghana**
6. Mason Edward Jireh (Ghana)
7. Mason Edward (Pastor), **Koforidua, Ghana**
8. Mason Joshua, **Koforidua, Ghana**
9. Mason Shirley Nana Akua (Mrs), **Koforidua, Ghana**
10. Mends Bridget Shevon **(D)**
11. Mends Raphael Edem Agboli, **USA**
12. Mends Sheila Maame Afua, **Accra, Ghana**
13. Mensah Bea (Abena Brempomaa), **USA**
14. Mensah Emmanuel Annor **(D)**
15. Mensah Maame Fosua, **Accra, Ghana**
16. Mensah Marony, **Accra, Ghana**
17. Mensah Mercy Asante, **Ghana**
18. Mensah-Mends Olive Lady (Mrs), **Accra, Ghana**
19. Minta-Aning Jaden, **Canada**
20. Minta-Aning Jeffrey, **Canada**
21. Minta-Aning Jesse, **Canada**

N

1. Nimako George Sena, **Ghana**
2. Nimako Jeremy Miles, **Ghana**
3. Nortey Imaa Agbemebiese (Mrs), **Accra, Ghana**
4. Nortey Naa Shorme, **London, UK**
5. Nortey Nii Nortei (D)
6. Nortey Philomena Ama (Mrs), **Accra, Ghana**
7. Nortey Sedinam, **Accra, Ghana**
8. Nortey Victor Okwei, **Accra, Ghana**
9. Nyadu-Addo Adriana, **Kumasi, Ghana**
10. Nyadu-Addo Charles Oti, **Germany**
11. Nyadu-Addo Dionne (Captain), **Kumasi, Ghana**
12. Nyadu-Addo Jerrold Benedict, **Kumasi Ghana**
13. Nyadu-Addo Kendra Akosua Takyiaw, **Kumasi, Ghana**
14. Nyadu-Addo Ralph (Dr) **Kumasi, Ghana**
15. Nyadu-Addo Russel Ralph John (Ghana)
16. Nyame Afia (Awo), **(D)**
17. Nyan Kwesi, **Ghana**
18. Nyan Ohene Kuuku, **Ghana**
19. Nyarkoa Emmanuella, **Ghana**
20. Nyarkoa Nana, **Canada**
21. Nyarkoah Laureen, **Ghana**

O

1. Obiri Yeboah, **Ghana**
2. Ocloo Bridget, **Nkawkaw, Ghana**
3. Ocloo Delian, **Nkawkaw, Ghana**
4. Ocloo Jesse, **Nkawkaw, Ghana**
5. Ocloo Joana, **Nkawkaw, Ghana**
6. Ocloo Joel, **Nkawkaw, Ghana**
7. Oduro Christiana, **Nkawkaw, Ghana)**
8. Ofori Ann-Phyllis (Mrs), **Corby, UK**
9. Ofori Jodie-Michelle, **Corby, UK**
10. Ofori Jonelle-Christie, **Corby, UK**
11. Ofori Samuel Kwaku (Rev), **Corby, UK**
12. Ofosu Leslie Yaw, **Obuasi, Ghana**
13. Okrah Irene Auntie Ama
14. Okrah Kwaku **(D)**
15. Okyere Aaron, **Koforidua, Ghana**
16. Okyere Anita, **Koforidua, Ghana**
17. Okyere Antoinette, **Koforidua, Ghana**
18. Okyere Audrey, **London UK**
19. Okyere Claudia, **London UK**
20. Okyere Eddie, **Ghana**
21. Okyere Emmanuel Baffour, **Koforidua, Ghana**
22. Okyere Georgina, **Koforidua, Ghana**
23. Okyere Gloria, **Koforidua, Ghana**
24. Okyere Grace, **London UK**
25. Okyere Josephine, **Koforidua, Ghana**
26. Okyere Kwasi **(D)**
27. Okyere Mary. **Koforidua, Ghana**
28. Okyere Mercy Rita, **Koforidua, Ghana**

29. Okyere Moses, **Koforidua, Ghana**
30. Okyere Raphael Yaw, **Koforidua, Ghana**
31. Okyere Tina Akua, **Ghana**
32. Okyere -Darko Margaret, **London, UK**
33. **Opanin Kwame Afram (JB Scatter), Akyeamehene (D)**
34. Oppong Daniel, **Ghana**
35. Oppong Emmanuel Kwasi, **Ghana**
36. Oppong Jennifer, **Ghana**
37. Oppong Sampson, **Koforidua, Ghana**
38. Oppong Theresa Akua **(D)**
39. Osei Adrielle, **Omaha, USA**
40. Osei Anthony Banier, **Koforidua, Ghana**
41. Osei Camille, **Omaha, USA**
42. Osei Cindy (Mrs), **Omaha, USA**
43. Osei Elian, **Omaha, USA**
44. Osei Gladys, **Ghana**
45. Osei Kwaku, **Ghana**
46. Osei Rosina (Adwoa Agyapomaa), **(D)**
47. Osei-Agyeman Michael, **Omaha, USA**
48. Osei-Boateng Michael, **Akim, Tafo, Ghana**
49. Ossei-Konadu Selina, **Akim Tafo, Ghana**
50. Ossei Alexandra Abrokwah (Mrs), **Slough, UK**
51. Ossei Alexcia, **London, UK**
52. Ossei Angelo, **London, UK**
53. Ossei Anthony, **London, UK**
54. Ossei Anthony Kwasi (Snr), **London, UK**
55. Ossei Catherine Juliana (Mrs), **London, UK**
56. Ossei Elizabeth Jane (Rev) **(D)**
57. Ossei George Kwaku **(D)**
58. Ossei Martin Kwadwo (Rev), **London, UK**
59. Ossei Matthew Anthomy, **London, UK**
60. Ossei Michael Kwadwo, **London, UK**
61. **Ossei Michael Kwasi (Master Ossei) (D)**
62. Ossei Naomi-Ruth Akua, **London, UK**
63. Ossei Olivia-Marie, **London, UK**
64. Ossei Patricia, **London, UK**
65. Ossei-Williams Alexcia, **Slough, UK**
66. Ossei-Williams Michael Kwasi (Rev), **Slough, UK**
67. Owuraku, **Ghana**
68. Boatemaa, **Ghana**
69. Owusu Adelaide Boamah, **(D)**
70. Owusu Agnes, **Osino, Ghana**
71. Owusu Agnes Yaa **(D)**
72. Owusu Anna Yaa Abon, **Kumasi, Ghana**
73. Owusu Anthony, **Accra, Ghana**
74. Owusu Anthony Kofi, **Accra, Ghana**
75. Owusu Augusta Abena, **Accra, Ghana**
76. Owusu Augustine Michael, **Koforidua, Ghana**
77. Owusu Dominic Kwadwo Asante, **New Tafo, Ghana**
78. Owusu Elsa Afua Dufie, **Kumasi, Ghana**
79. Owusu Gladys Amponsah, **New Tafo, Ghana**
80. Owusu Isaac (Pastor), **Koforidua, Ghana**
81. Owusu James Atta Kakra, **Ghana**
82. Owusu James Atta Panin, **Ghana**
83. Owusu Josephine Gertrude Afua (Dr, Mrs), **Brampton, Canada**
84. Owusu Kelvin Dogbe, **Akim Osino, Ghana**
85. Owusu Kwabena Boamah, **Akim Tafo, Ghana**
86. Owusu Lucinda Takyiaw, **Osino, Ghana**
87. Owusu Michael Kwadwo, **Accra, Ghana**
88. Owusu Michael Kwasi **(D)**
89. Owusu Neal Kwesi, **Brampton, Canada**
90. Owusu Osei Yaw, **Brampton Canada**
91. Owusu Philomena, **Osino, Ghana**
92. Owusu Raphael Yaw, **New Tafo, Ghana**
93. Owusu Regina Akosua Abon, **Kumasi, Ghana**
94. Owusu Regina Amma **(D)**
95. Owusu Regina Mida, **Osino, Ghana**
96. Owusu Samuel Danquah, **Akim Tafo, Ghana**
97. Owusu Tracey Obaa Yaa, **Brampton, Canada**
98. Owusu Vivian Amma **(D)**
99. Owusu Yeboah Christiana, **Accra, Ghana**
100. Owusua Comfort, **Akim Tafo, Ghana**
101. Owusua Docia, **Ghana**
102. Owusu-Ansah Albert Kwadwo, **London, UK**
103. Owusu-Ansah Irene Afua Ossei (Mrs), **London, UK**
104. Owusu-Ansah Albert Jnr, **Milton Keynes, UK**
105. Owusu-Ansah Maa Fia, **London, UK**
106. Owusu-Ansah Paa Sei, **Maryland, USA**

107. Owusu-Agyemang Anthony, **Italy**
108. Owusu Agyeman Benedetta**, Italy**
109. Owusu-Agyeman Maxwell, **Italy**
110. Owusu-Agyeman Nana, **Ghana**
111. Owusu-Boamah Adelaide **(D)**
112. Owusu-Dankwa Rosemond, **New Tafo, Ghana**
113. Owusu-Frempong Samuel (Rev Fr) **(D)**
114. Owusu-Frempong Samuel (Ghana)
115. Owusu-Twum Afriyie Ofosua, **Philadelphia, USA**
116. Owusu-Twum Jeanette (Mrs), **Philadelphia, USA**
117. Owusu-Twum Maxwell (Pastor), **Philadelphia, USA**
118. Owusu-Twum Nshiraba Ossei, **Philadelphia, USA**
119. Oyo Naa, **Ghana**

P

1. **Pokua Ama Nana (D) (family matriarch)**

R

1. Reinduls Elizabeth Akua **(D)**
2. Reinduls Veronica Afia **(D)**
3. Robinson- Matthews Audrey (Mrs), **London, UK**
4. Robinson-Matthews Ezra, London, UK
5. Robinson-Matthews Jeremiah, **London, UK**
6. Robinson-Matthews Sienna, **London, UK**

S

1. Saheeb Amara Azaria, **London, UK**
2. Saheeb Billal Omone, **London, UK**
3. Saheeb Felicity Akosua (Mrs), **London, UK**
4. Saheeb Makayla Emikele, **London, UK**
5. Saheeb Sara Ayana, **London, UK**
6. Sammy Kofi, **Ghana**
7. Sarpong Agnes Takyiaw Addo, **Ghana**
8. Sarpong Brenda Abena, **Ghana**
9. Selby Love, **Ghana**

T

1. Takyiaw Maame Yaa Wendy, **Switzerland**
2. **Takyiaw Yaa (Maame Panin), (D)**
3. Tetteh Anita, **Ghana**
4. Tetteh Eric Yaw Korade **(D)**
5. Tetteh Richmond Kwaku **(D)**
6. Tetteh Thomas Kofi, **Ghana**

W

1. Walker Victor Kofi, **Ghana**

Y

1. Yamoah Kwaku, **UK**

Printed in the United States
by Baker & Taylor Publisher Services